DIAMOND IN THE ROUGH

The Dave Clark Story

To Gene,

Dream and do.

Best wishes always,

Dave Clark

4

DIAMOND IN THE ROUGH

The Dave Clark Story

As told to Roger Neumann

Diamond in the Rough
The Dave Clark Story

Cover design and photo editing by Ron Lindensmith

Printed in the United States of America

www.DaveClarkBaseball.com

We dedicate this book, with love …

From Dave:

To my wife, Camilla, and our children, Elicia and Trey.
To my parents, Lillian and Bernard.
And to my brothers, Dan and Doug.

From Roger:

To my wife, Nancy; our daughter, Michelle; and our sons, Mark and Scott.
To my sisters, Barbara and Doris.
And to the memory of my parents, Amelia and Alwin.

Contents

Foreword

The first time I met Dave Clark was in 1990 in Pompano Beach, Florida. A simple man being escorted by a beautiful woman who was introduced to me as Camilla. I remember thinking, "Here is a guy who gets it. A man who reminds me of my father."

Dave Clark was on crutches, but you hardly noticed. You noticed the eyes first. The steely determination mixed with a certain gentle quality. The mouth, which was a crooked grin—the smile seemed to go on forever.

As we chatted, he told me a remarkable story about a more remarkable life. His life. Struck by polio at ten months, he simply refused to be restrained by his condition. He forgot not to achieve but reached for the exceptional.

Over the years, we have stayed in touch. Very much the way you are reading this. We wrote letters. Warm letters. Formal letters. Probing letters. Yes, even once, angry letters. Nothing remarkable, just two friends relating the experiences that go with the passage of time.

Dave Clark's story is an astonishing blend of fact and fact. It only reads like fiction, but one could never make up the battles he has waged, the obstacles he has overcome, the victories that were finally his.

Everyone of every age will find something in this book to hold onto. Young, old, player, observer. You will be moved because real life is like that. It is moving.

Read this book and wonder, "Could I do that?" Read it and celebrate the human spirit. Reflect and marvel at the dignity of man, the strength of character, the ultimate joy of a life well lived.

My favorite part of the book? That's easy. Remember that beautiful woman? Well, Dave married her, proving he's not as dumb as I have sometimes accused him of being. Then they went and had a beautiful child so that this wonderful story couldn't help but have a happy ending.

I'm just glad I got a peek or two inside. You'll be glad, too.

Mike Veeck

Preface

I thought I knew Dave Clark. After having written several newspaper articles and a few columns about him, I figured I'd pretty much covered the basic story of his life. But each time we sat down together to delve into another fascinating piece of that wonderful story for this book, I realized how wrong I was.

I barely knew Dave at all. Oh, sure, I was quite familiar with the fact that he'd had polio as an infant, that his growth had been stunted and he'd had to use crutches to get around all his life and that, despite everything, he'd gone on to play, manage, coach and scout in professional baseball. Those of us who knew even that much about him were awed by all he's accomplished. But there's so much more to the man, and to his life. And as I learned the many little stories behind the big story, I became even more amazed at what he's done. I hope this book will leave you feeling the same way.

I'm pleased and honored to have been Dave's teammate in the telling of this very inspirational story. I want to thank him publicly now for that opportunity, and also for the many detailed notes and written accounts he provided, plus the many stimulating conversations we shared, as this book came together. I found Dave's ability to recall names, dates, places and events no less amazing than his many other accomplishments.

Roger Neumann

Introduction: Game Over

It was early evening, cold and gray outside. From my motel room window, I looked out onto Montreal, blanketed in a fresh layer of snow that was illuminated only by the last slanting rays of a sinking sun and the headlights of the cars that moved slowly along the wide street below. All the windows in the tall buildings along the street were dark, as were the street lights and traffic signals.

Electrical power was out throughout the area. First reports from the oldies station I picked up on my transistor radio indicated the blackout might be related to an earthquake that had rumbled through there the day before, but as it turned out that wasn't the case. Whatever the reason, my room was getting colder and darker by the minute as I sat there looking out on that wintry scene.

The conditions matched my mood. This was the first day of a trip I'd been planning for some time, and I should have been enjoying it. But I felt lousy. I had a persistent cough, frequent migraine headaches and occasional chills, and in general I hurt everywhere—my eyes, my ears, my back, my knees, you name it. Even my skin ached. What's more, I'd been sleeping poorly lately and I had little appetite.

Just as disturbing, if not more so, my personality was undergoing a change. I didn't recognize or particularly like this new Dave Clark, but there didn't seem to be anything I could do to stop or even slow the change. Normally, I'm a happy-go-lucky guy who enjoys life and takes it as it comes. But now I was sullen, irritable and cranky. The enthusiasm seemed to have been drained out of me, and I was withdrawn and more self-centered than usual. While I recognized this was happening, I felt powerless to stop it.

"I'm not myself, that's for sure," I wrote at one point in a journal I kept on that trip. During certain periods of my life—I guess when I needed to do some soul-searching or when I wanted to record changes in my physical condition for later reference—I would find a spiral notebook or just some sheets of scrap paper and begin jotting down my thoughts or feelings, or take note of how my body was reacting. These ramblings served me well later, when I began looking back at my life and sought confirmation of what I remembered, or clarification for what I could no longer recall clearly.

Two things had triggered my physical and mental decline at this time. One, I was in the early stages of a debilitating condition called post-polio syndrome, in which the muscles of the body of someone who had polio decades ago begin to break down from years of use—and, in my case, you might say, abuse. And two, I was suffering from a withdrawal from baseball, my professional playing career having just ended a few months before at the age of thirty-five.

Anyway, I was there in Montreal and I was determined to see this trip through. It would be ten days of watching hockey, with a little Canadian football thrown in. And a lot of driving, too—2,281 miles of it, to be exact, by the time I got back home in Corning, New York.

It was to be a vacation, but also a time for reflection. A time to look back over an unlikely career as an athlete for a guy who had developed polio as an infant—this was in the days just before the Salk vaccine became available—and was basically given up for dead by our family doctor. It was a time to remember those glory days when I played in the minor leagues, a guy of five-foot-two pitching a knuckleball that I had taught myself—from crutches, by the way, which is how I batted, too, and of course fielded. And the days before that, when I played all the sports with all the kids in the neighborhood, and even made it into Little League, and later played club hockey as a goalie in college, and club baseball, and a few years later coached a college varsity baseball team. When I barnstormed around the country with the Indianapolis Clowns as a player in the 1970s and again in the '80s, and later as a combination player and part-owner. And when I nearly made it to the major leagues, and wouldn't that have been something?

That part of my life ended after the baseball season of 1988. The post-polio syndrome was slowly but surely wearing my body down, and I could no longer summon the energy or the skills that I needed to play the game at the professional level. It was during spring training with the Clowns that year that I realized it was time to walk away from baseball, but I decided to play out that season. I owed it to myself to do that, and I felt I owed it to the Clowns.

I remember clearly the day I knew it was over. It was March 19, 1988, a blindingly sunny day in Ocala, Florida. I was fielding ground balls at first base during infield practice. As always, I was positioned fairly close to the bag, the crutches tucked up under my arms, my glove held low to the ground and my body coiled and ready to spring into action. At the crack of the bat, I lunged for a ball that was hit sharply to my right, tumbling to the infield dirt as my crutches fell to either side of me and the ball slithered past my glove into right field. I lay there for a moment, disappointed that I had missed the ball but also suddenly aware that the old bounce wasn't in me anymore. Instead of springing back up, as I had done countless times before, I struggled to stand again. I fumbled with my crutches, straining with every ounce of strength in my arms to push myself back to my feet.

I became aware, then and there, that my body was trying to tell me something and that I had no choice but to listen and accept what it was saying. It was saying: It's over, buddy; time to go now. To be honest, my body had probably been saying that for a long time, but my heart wouldn't let me listen. Now I couldn't ignore it any longer.

I dusted off my uniform, stalling a bit, trying to sort out the confusing messages I was receiving, not sure of what the next step was to be. At the plate, my good friend Sal Tombasco was ready to bounce another one my way and was watching me anxiously, a fungo bat on one hand and a scuffed-up practice ball in the other.

"Okay, here we go. Get one," Sal called out. "Comin' your way, Dave." Or something like that.

I heard his voice but really wasn't listening. All activity on the field seemed to have stopped, and I sensed that everyone was watching me, waiting for me to get myself set. Without a word, I turned and slowly walked down the right field line, my head hung low, my vision clouded by tears that welled up in my eyes.

That afternoon I drove out into the woods nearby and found a place to park where I could be alone. I needed to think, to reflect. I knew it was over then, or soon would be. There was no way I could keep up the training, the practice, the travel and the games. Hard as it was, I came to a decision then and there: I'd play out the season, but no more after that. And then, as I sat there alone in my car, all that I had accomplished over the years came back to me in a flood of memories, and I cried over my loss.

I made the last out for the Clowns that season, grounding to third in a game at Charlotte, North Carolina, on August 14, 1988. It was not only my last at-bat as a player but also the last out in the history of the Clowns.

We packed away all that was left of the Clowns—the uniforms and costumes, the equipment, some posters and other memorabilia from an era gone by. It wasn't until many years later that I learned our team, which had long ago been integrated, was the last surviving member of the old Negro Leagues. The legendary Satchel Paige and home run king Hank Aaron had worn the uniform.

That day in 1988, though, we went quietly, with no fanfare—for the Clowns or for Dave Clark. With one final swing of the bat, one little piss-ant ground ball to third base, I closed out my playing career, the Indianapolis Clowns franchise and the history of the Negro Leagues. Strike one, strike two and strike three. Game over.

I thought it was the end of my career in professional sports, not just my playing career. My body ached and my spirits were low. I knew I would never play again, and I could not see a future for me in baseball or any other game.

Playing is what had driven me all my life, and playing is all I had ever wanted to do. It was all I *could* do, or so I thought. I never considered what other opportunities might be out there for someone who knew baseball, wanted badly to stay in the game and was willing to work hard to do so.

As I embarked on my trip through Canada a few months later, I wondered and worried about what I would do with the rest of my life.

Hell, I was three weeks shy of thirty-six—still a young man outside the world of professional sports. There had to be *something* I could do.

To be honest, though, I didn't feel young. I sensed that I had lost my youth along with my playing career, and that realization left me feeling desperate. An athlete, after all, is really living an extended period of his youth. He or she tends to stay younger mentally, or maybe it's just that a life in sports slows down the maturation process and that athletes are really less mature than the rest of the population. I don't know. What I do know is that when I really *was* young I thought I'd be able to play forever. Well, forever came plenty fast.

Now, with my life as an athlete behind me, I was beginning to wonder just how much more of life I had ahead of me. I didn't think there was much. In my journal, I wrote that I doubted I would live to be forty. And that was just four years away!

This is what I wrote near the end of that trip to Canada:

"My body and health are going downhill rapidly. I really don't believe I have much time left on Earth. Not only don't I feel good, I feel old. I look in the mirror and I feel I've aged very rapidly in the last couple of years. I'm not adjusting very well to not being young anymore."

When I came across that journal not too long before I started working on this book, I was shocked to find just how low my physical health and mental state had sunk during that time. I could remember being depressed for a time, but I had forgotten how difficult a period that was for me. The journal entries did not read like me at all. It was as if those words had come from someone else, someone I didn't know.

Since that time, I've come to understand that life is a series of changes, both good and bad, and that we all go through the ups and downs. The downs can be severe, but we must work our way through them and get our lives back on track. No matter how down we are, we have to find a way to dig ourselves up out of the hole we're in and get back on level ground. Fortunately, I've always been able to do that.

At the time of my Canada trip, though, I couldn't see past that difficult point in my life. I couldn't get myself back on track, on level ground. I couldn't visualize a future in which I wasn't an athlete.

I had no way of knowing a whole new life would soon open up for me.

CHAPTER 1:

BEATING THE ODDS

I was born September 6, 1952, in Corning Hospital, the first of three children—all boys—of Lillian and Bernard Clark. Apparently healthy at birth, I became ill the following June. I ran a high fever and I cried a lot—at least that's how my dad remembers it.

Our family doctor told my parents I had measles, but my condition only got worse, and after three weeks I had lost the use of muscles all over my body. I was paralyzed on my left side.

My parents took me to the doctor again, and this time his diagnosis was right on the money: I had polio.

At first, the doctor told my parents there was little chance that I'd live. Then he said I might live, but if I did I'd most likely be a vegetable. That's how he put it: a vegetable.

Dad remembers: "That was a real shock. Dave was our first child, and we had great expectations for him."

Dad recalls Mom saying, "Oh, doctor, if he can just walk."

"No, Mrs. Clark," the doctor said. "It's much more important if we find out he has no brain damage. If he can just use his mind."

And he was right. My mind was what was really important. Without the mind I possess, I know my body never would have been able to get me to the places I've been. Being able to anticipate, to think ahead and focus on a task until it's completed satisfactorily—that's what separates successful people from the rest, and I've had that.

Dream and do it: That's the blueprint I've followed. Don't get me wrong—I don't consider myself a dreamer. There are dreamers and then there are people who pursue their dreams with conviction and passion, who keep working toward a goal until they reach it, who prove to themselves and to others that dreams *do* come true. That's me.

Baseball might be the ultimate dream world, and so I guess it suited me. Who doesn't remember being a kid and dreaming of hitting the game-winning grand slam in the final game of the World Series, or coming out of the bullpen to strike out the big hitter with the bases loaded? As kids, we don't know yet that these dreams are just on loan to us, to be lived in and enjoyed only for the moment. Most of the time, when a boy or girl becomes a teenager, reality sets in and the dreams begin to fade. Only a precious few of us get to live out our dreams.

Since I was a kid, I'd never been content just to participate. I've always been a take-charge guy, an organizer and a leader, and that's because I had the mind even if I didn't have the legs. I've been able to think through a situation thoroughly, and to gauge the impact a decision will have—not just on me but on others as well. Life, after all, is just a series of decisions. The trick is to make more good decisions than bad ones. I've been able to do that, though of course none of us had any idea what lay ahead for me that fateful day when the doctor delivered the terrible news to my parents.

I was just ten months old at the time—unable to move my legs, or my arms, and not yet able to make any but the most basic decisions. This was about two and a half years before the Salk polio vaccine became available, so there was no way to prevent the disease. And there was no known cure for polio, either, and no effective treatment. The Salk vaccine, which was approved for public use on April 12, 1955, effectively eliminated polio in most of the world. But even today, there is no known effective treatment.

I spent two or three weeks at Corning Hospital, where nurses regularly wrapped my arms and legs in hot packs. Then, in July, I was transferred to the Ithaca Reconstruction Home in Ithaca, New York, about forty miles northeast of where we lived. By then I could move only the muscles in my right arm, and those just a little.

When my parents dropped me off, the superintendent of the home asked them to stop in her office before they left. They did, both of them in tears, and what she told them did nothing to lift their spirits. The woman said Mom and Dad shouldn't expect much improvement in my condition during my stay there, and that it was unlikely I would ever walk, even with crutches. She was telling them this, she said, so as not to get their hopes up. It had that effect, too, but just for a little while.

Dad remembers: "Your mom and I cried all through that meeting and all the way home. The woman was very good, but when she talked to us she was very harsh about it."

I spent eleven months at the home in Ithaca. Dad was working three jobs in those days to make ends meet, but he would still find time to drive up to see me once a week. Mom quit her job as a secretary at what was then Corning Glass Works (now Corning Incorporated) and made the forty-five-minute drive to Ithaca three times a week.

My parents' visits lasted two to three hours. They weren't supposed to take me off the premises, but occasionally they would sneak me out and drive to nearby Stewart Park for a picnic. I suppose they just wanted to be doing something "normal" with me. But they were found out one day when I gave up the evidence. Dad had fed me hot dogs on one of those picnics, and after returning to the home I got sick and vomited.

I became attached to one of the nurses who cared for me. Dad said the woman called Mom a couple of times to ask if she could take me to her home for dinner, and my mother always gave her consent. Mom probably never thought much of it, but eventually she began to notice that the nurse and I had become close. Dad said it tore her up inside to watch this relationship developing. Still, he remembered Mom saying she'd rather have that situation than see me being cared for by a mean nurse I didn't like.

It's funny, but today I have absolutely no memory of that nurse or the time we spent together. In fact, I cannot recall a single thing about that reconstruction home or the people who worked or lived there. As I began working on this book, I visited the home again for the fist time since I'd stayed there, thinking it might rekindle some memories, but no. Nothing.

One winter evening back then, on her drive home from Ithaca, Mom was involved in a three-car crash. It happened on Route 13, a two-lane highway that winds through the countryside south from Ithaca to state Route 17 (now Interstate 86) in Horseheads.

Mom was alone in a practically new Oldsmobile, one of four southbound vehicles traveling in a pack. The trailing car passed the other three and then made a sharp right-hand turn into a driveway, causing a pileup behind it. Mom's car, the middle of the three, was totaled but, thankfully, she wasn't badly hurt. She suffered from whiplash and an elbow injury but wasn't hospitalized and didn't miss a visit with me. Dad said the next time she showed up at the home, though, Mom was driving her father's car.

Many years later, my mother told me that by all accounts of the experts, I shouldn't be here, that it was a miracle I lived at all. She said it always made her feel that God had a great purpose for my life. In any form, life is a miracle, she said, and mine particularly so. I like to think she was right.

Despite the dire warnings when I first arrived at the Ithaca Reconstruction Home, I made significant improvement over the eleven months I stayed there. But that was as far as the staff thought they could take me. One day they sent me home with instructions for my parents on exercises, physical therapy and massage treatments. I walked out of there that day with tiny braces on my legs and a small pair of crutches tucked under my arms. But I was walking when I left. *Walking!*

Already I was beating the odds.

Three times a week until I started school, Mom took me to a physical therapy program at the Booth Elementary School in Elmira. I also followed an exercise routine at home. I did pull-ups on a bar that hung in the doorway between rooms. Lying on the floor and grabbing onto Dad's arm, I did sit-ups. And I did a series of range-of-motion drills that worked my arms and legs.

Little did I know it at the time, but I was starting on the course for a lifetime of physical conditioning. And the pull-ups, or chin-ups, would help me to develop a powerful upper body that would serve me well throughout my life, and certainly throughout my career in sports.

My dad gave me nightly rubdowns. He'd help me stretch out on the living room floor and then would rub my legs with olive oil or some other lotion. I hated the oily feeling it left on my legs, and to this day I don't like to have lotions of any kind rubbed on me, especially if I can't bathe or shower afterwards.

It's the same with my hair. Mom used to gather us boys—my brothers Dan and Doug and me—on Sunday mornings and dress us up in our finest clothes and then work a big glob of Vitalis or Brylcreem into our hair before we headed off to the Christian Missionary Alliance Church just across the street from our house. I couldn't stand that greasy feeling on my head. Ever since I outgrew that, I've never put anything on my hair except water.

The exercises and rubdowns got to be pretty routine after a while. But one night when Dad was rubbing some lotion onto my legs something weird happened. A woman from the neighborhood walked in—just came through the front door without knocking, which was unusual—and saw us there on the floor. She immediately took over for Dad, but as she rubbed my legs she prayed to God to heal me, in a voice that was as strange as her behavior. Dad and I just looked at each other, not sure what to make of it.

Fortunately, the woman's husband showed up before long. He was clearly embarrassed, and he whisked her away and led her back home. Later, I learned the woman had wound up in a mental institution.

Having parents who were so devoted to me and so helpful made all the difference in my physical development. I needed them in those early years and was insecure when they weren't around. I remember that when Mom drove Dad to work at the Ingersoll-Rand plant (now Dresser-Rand) in Painted Post just before seven o'clock every morning, I would watch from an upstairs window as they rode away. Then I'd wait there, crying, until I saw Mom's car pull into the driveway ten or fifteen minutes later, and I'd crawl back into bed before she could come inside and catch me.

Two things were happening now that would stay with me all my life. One, I was developing the belief that I couldn't allow anyone to detect a weakness in me of any kind. Two, because of the strength I drew from my parents' love, I was becoming fiercely independent.
I still have those qualities today.

CHAPTER 2:

MY SAVIORS

My childhood was the best.

We lived on East William Street in Corning, in a neighborhood of hard-working blue-collar, lower middle class people. There were lots of kids around my age, and something was going on all the time, usually involving sports. It was a great place to grow up in the 1950s and '60s.

Until I got into second grade, though, I didn't participate in any sports, either in school or around the neighborhood. Teachers never let me join in any physical activities in school, and I guess I just never felt I'd fit in on the playgrounds and ball fields at home. When the games started in gym or other classes, teachers always told me to go and sit somewhere on the side, where I wouldn't get hurt—and, of course, where I wouldn't get an opportunity to see if I *could* participate.

There was one teacher, though, who didn't seem to consider whether or not I could participate in something that she probably didn't even think of as a physical activity. Well, for her and the other kids, maybe it wasn't. But a walk of several blocks for a six-year-old on crutches with full-length braces on both legs was not only an activity, it was a chore. And that's what I found myself facing one day in first grade at the Hugh Gregg Elementary School.

A feeling of horror shot through me when our teacher announced to the class that we were going to take our first field trip, in about a week, to the Corning Northside Fire Department. The firehouse was four or five blocks away, and we would be walking. *Walking?!* Would I be able to do that? Would I be able to keep up with the other kids? Could I go that far without taking a break? Worse, if I did need a break, would the teacher make the other kids stop and wait for me?

I hadn't yet gained the acceptance of the other kids through sports, and I was still noticing some of them staring at me from time to time. Those looks and the fact that I couldn't go places as fast as them disturbed me greatly. The last thing I wanted now was something that would make me stand out any more than I already did. So, day by day over the next week, my anxiety grew as the date of the field trip drew near. I kept waiting for our teacher to tell me she'd made special arrangements for me to get to the fire hall, but she never did.

Finally, the day arrived. And so did my young "savior," as I now think of him. Little Ernie Pound, one of my classmates, had brought his red Radio Flyer wagon to school that day, with the sole intention of giving me a ride to the fire hall. The teacher gave Ernie the okay as we lined up for the trip, and I hopped in the wagon. My classmates accepted the wagon, and even helped make it a fun experience for me, asking to take turns pulling me. And, for all my concern, the field trip turned out just fine.

From then on, Ernie Pound would bring his wagon to school anytime we had a walking field trip scheduled. I've sometimes wondered how a boy so young could have been so wise—wiser, even, than my teacher. I haven't seen Ernie in many years, and I have no idea where he is today or what he's doing. And I don't remember if I ever really thanked him for what he did for me, but I guess I probably didn't. So, Ernie, let me take this opportunity to do so.

You may not have realized it at the time, but you were my young savior when I needed one desperately. Without you and your wagon, I just don't know how I would have gotten through what surely would have been some very difficult and probably very embarrassing experiences.

From the bottom of my heart, Ernie, thank you so much.

A man named Bill Schnetzler saved me in his own way. My second-grade gym teacher at Gregg Elementary, he had as profound an impact on my life as anyone aside from my parents. In Mr. Schnetzler's class I became, for the first time, just one of the boys. And because of him, I began playing sports not only in gym class but outside school as well.

Mr. Schnetzler obviously recognized that I was in some ways different from the other kids, and he didn't put me in positions that would embarrass me or risk injury to me. But he didn't see my physical limitations as a reason for me not to be part of the fun of gym class—and for me it always was fun, from that point on. Mr. Schnetzler included me in everything.

"Look, I want you to at least try this," he would say. And I always did, gladly and eagerly.

The first time it happened was when Mr. Schnetzler gathered all the boys to explain how he wanted each of us to climb the ropes that hung from the ceiling of the gym. Kids were exchanging *who, me?* glances as I turned and began walking away.

"Hold it there," Mr.Schnetzler said. "Where are you going?"

"I … I'm just going …"

"You're just going to try this like everybody else," he said.

I went back to the group, and one by one the boys started climbing the ropes. It seemed like a long way to the top, and I guess it was. Nobody made it all the way, some never even got off the floor, and a few fell to the padded mat below. Then it was my turn.

I'd never really stopped to consider how all those exercises at home had strengthened my upper body. Pull-ups, push-ups and the rest—they bulked up my arms, my shoulders, my chest and my back. I needed those muscles just to propel myself on crutches all day, and using them seemed natural to me. But without realizing it, I had developed powerful muscles where most kids hadn't worked theirs at all.

I gripped the rope tightly and began climbing, hand over hand. I couldn't use my feet to hold on the way the other kids could, but that was okay. I didn't need them. I made it to the top without really much effort, then came back down. When I turned to the group, I saw kids with this *Wow!* look on their faces. They were amazed.

I was the only boy in the class to reach the top of the ropes that day. For doing so, I was awarded a free ice cream bar. And after that, kids never looked at me the same way again. They saw me as somebody with an ability that none of them had, these so-called able-bodied kids. They began treating me with a new respect, and I began having more self-confidence. I was a changed person from that day on.

I never sat out a gym activity again. I never again waited in a corner or watched from the sidelines while the other kids played and laughed and enjoyed themselves. When they played, I played. Now I was one of them.

The next year, with Mr. Schnetzler again my gym teacher, we played softball. He'd have us hit from a tee, and I was pretty good at it. I already loved baseball from watching it on TV and listening on the radio, and it was fun to actually play the game.

"I remember the crutches but I don't remember ever seeing him as handicapped," Peggie Stinson, a schoolmate and friend, remembered many years later. "He never ceased to awe me. I'll never forget the first time I saw him step up to home plate. I remember thinking, well, he deserves a chance, at least. To my amazement, he not only hit the ball, he walloped it and sent it sailing."

Pretty soon, I was playing everything the other boys around the neighborhood were playing, too. And my natural leadership qualities began to take over. I became not just another player but the leader of the pack. More often than not, I was the one who scheduled the next game, made sure we had the right equipment and enough players, set down the rules and generally took charge.

I guess you could say I might have benefited from some management training, though. My temper sometimes got in the way. I remember one time trying to talk one of the kids, John Potter, into playing a game of baseball. We just *had* to have him to even up the sides. John kept saying no, he couldn't play and that was final. I had a ball in my hand and, without thinking, I threw it at him and hit him in the face. He got a bloody lip and ran to my house to tell my mother. When I got home, Mom pulled out the belt she used to administer discipline, and whacked me good.

Maybe my behavior was a little over the top, but we were kids and, yeah, I had a bit of a temper. Well, I still do, but I hope I've learned to control it a little better than that.

The point is that Mr. Schnetzler had convinced me—or let me convince myself—that if I tried something I just might be able to do it. He didn't force me to do anything, but he gave me the opportunity to try everything. And that's all I ever really needed or wanted: an opportunity. I've been trying everything ever since.

Many years later, while doing research for this book, we caught up with another former teacher of mine, Marjorie Wheeler. I had Mrs. Wheeler for both fifth grade and sixth, because she moved up when I did.

Mrs. Wheeler was eighty-eight years old and living in a retirement home in Texas when we talked with her, but she had no trouble remembering me. She recalled a quiet, small kid who was carried into her room by his mother every day. She said somebody made a box for me so I could rest my feet on it because they didn't reach the floor.

Mrs. Wheeler remembered that I couldn't wait for recess every day so I could go outside and play, especially baseball.

"That child simply loved sports," she said. "He was always right there at home plate. And, dear God, it used to scare me to death. I always thought he'd get hurt, but he never did."

She remembered that I could play, too: "Boy, he could hit that ball, I'll tell you that."

Mrs. Wheeler said she followed my career and marveled at my success.

"I've been amazed at the progress he's made in his life," she said. And: "I've always admired his determination. He was determined he was going to take part in sports, and baseball has been his whole life."

I'm sad to say that Mrs. Wheeler passed away in 2005. May she rest in peace.

We kids in the neighborhood played all the sports, whatever was in season, but baseball was the first game I learned and the one I most enjoyed playing.

Dad taught me how to play. He'd finish his shift at the Ingersoll-Rand plant at three every afternoon and get a ride from a co-worker to the corner of Bridge and East William streets, a block and a half from our house. Starting when I was around six years old, I'd wait for him at the corner, two baseball gloves and a ball in my hands, my legs wrapped in steel braces, and crutches under my arms. We'd walk home together, talking over our day. Then we'd play catch in the driveway for a half-hour or more, until Dad had to go inside to eat and then start on his other jobs, selling Fuller brushes and magazines door-to-door.

One afternoon something happened that helped set the course for the rest of my life. Dad and I were playing catch, and he was tossing pop flies to me. I misjudged one and it bounced off my forehead, knocking me to the ground. I lay there crying, and Dad walked over slowly and surveyed the situation. He could see that I wasn't badly hurt.

"Okay," he said. "Now, let's try that again."

Dad could have decided that was enough, that he didn't want his little boy with crutches to get hurt. He could have said baseball was too dangerous for me. He could have said no to sports, but he didn't.

What he did instead laid the foundation for any success I would enjoy from that moment on. You get knocked down, you get up—that was a motto I played by and lived by. I'd set a goal and do all I could to reach it. I understood that I would continue to get knocked down—we all get knocked down—but I was determined to keep getting up until I found myself staring my goal in the face.

Looking back, Mom and Dad were never overly protective. They never held me back from trying any activity that I wanted to try. In fact, they encouraged me at every step along the way.

Dad even made me a three-wheel electric cart to help me get around, and a fairly crude go-kart, both of which I drove myself. I frequently used one or the other to go to a game or practice, and I guess I was a bit reckless. Often I'd take a turn too fast, tip over the three-wheeler and send crutches, baseball equipment and myself spilling every which way.

Today I'm a pretty good driver—of a car or van, and even a scooter. For a long time, I resisted efforts to get me into a scooter or wheelchair, even at my doctor's strong suggestion that I do so to ease the stress on my body as I get older and the post-polio condition progresses. Finally I gave in, and now I regularly use a scooter to get around.

The van I drive is specially equipped to allow me to work the brake pedal by hand. As I get older, I find I use the van and my scooter more often than most people use their vehicles. Post-polio fatigue has convinced me it doesn't pay—in fact, it's foolish—to walk if I can ride.

Mom taught me how to drive. At first, I used full hand controls to operate both the brakes and the accelerator. But I found I could work the gas pedal with my foot, so after I passed my driver's test (full controls were mandated for me), I had that part disconnected and used just the hand brake.

The cart Dad made for me when I was a child gave me another level of independence. Suddenly, I was able to go farther faster, and I could easily haul all the equipment I needed, and more, to our games. That's the kind of thing Mom and Dad did for me all through my formative years, and well beyond. I could never have made it without them, and I will always be grateful for the love and support they gave me and the faith they showed in me, time and time again.

CHAPTER 3:

A BORN LEADER

The Clark house was the hub of activities for kids from all the neighborhood families—the De Primos, the Potters and the Cooks, the Moshiers, Cavallaros and Pettingills, the Lewises, Messinas and Ferraras.

I've always been organized, and an organizer, and it was true even then. I organized leagues for every sport we played and kept schedules and statistics and records, which I still have in boxes in the house where I live today. The Bic pen I scribbled notes or stats with was as much a part of my equipment as a ball or glove or bat.

My brother Dan once said, "Dave had to keep the most meticulous records in the history of kids' sport—batting averages, ERA's, innings pitched, goals, assists, touchdowns, shooting averages, etc. Whatever sport we were playing, Dave kept the records. If he hadn't worked in baseball, he could have worked for the Elias Sports Bureau as a statistician."

I even organized teams and leagues for the board games and card games I played, and the games I made up. I'd name teams for different cities, and players for each team (I always played for Corning). More often than not, my team would win, but once in a while I'd fix it so another team would win. From time to time, the schedule would take my team on the road, and then my bed at home would become a bunk on a train—I've always been fascinated by trains.

Anyway, Dan and I always had teams of our own in those sandlot games we played—each of us a team captain—and kids who were left over were formed into other teams. Dan, who was two and a half years younger than me, played all the sports. Doug, who was five years younger than me, never played with us, but boy, he sure could talk a good game.

His whole life, Doug has marched to the beat of a different drummer. When it came to sports, he really didn't have the hand-eye coordination, and I think he knew it. So as a kid, he went his own way when we got up a game.

"Nah, I'm not playing," he'd say. "I could kick your asses, but I've got better things to do."

"Come on," we'd say. "Kick our asses. Show us how good you are."

But he'd just walk away and go do his own thing, whatever that was.

Sometimes we'd taunt him, trying to get him to play, so we could kick *his* ass. And he could get kind of crazy. He'd come running after us, sometimes with a weapon—a hammer, a hose, even a pitchfork.

One winter night when my parents were away, Doug locked Dan and me and some friends of ours out of the house. He chased us with a hammer and drove us outside into the freezing cold with no coats on. We scattered and took cover behind bushes, cars and neighbors' houses. After a little while, another friend who hadn't been with us came down the street, went up to our house and rang the bell. Doug opened the door and whacked the kid in the head with the hammer. Crazy.

Dan was quite different. He was athletic, eventually growing to about six-two with a muscular build and long brownish-red hair. (Doug, who grew to about six feet tall, was a skinny kid, with long black hair.) When I mention the games I played as a kid, assume that Dan was there, a part of it all, but that Doug was not. That's usually how it was.

When the De Primo family moved to Elmira, about 20 miles away, we put a team in that city. Then, once a season Mom would pile all the kids from our neighborhood into the family station wagon and drive us to Elmira, where we'd play baseball or football all day while Mom visited with Mrs. De Primo. And once a season, Mrs. De Primo would load the Elmira kids into her car and visit us for a day.

Many years later, Mark De Primo recalled:

"Dave was coaching 'the gang' in Corning as early as I can remember. He organized all the games, put us in our positions, decided batting lineups and set up offensive and defensive alignments during our football games. During our baseball games, Dave usually pitched or played first base, would bat and at times would insist on running out his hits using his crutches to guide him up the base path. In football, he would be the quarterback. And it would not be unusual for Dave to fend you off with one of his crutches when you attempted to tackle him. I don't think he enjoyed being tackled, but he always insisted on being treated the same as everyone else on the field. Even at an early age, Dave understood the rules and execution of plays better than most people much older than him."

We kids had some god-awful disagreements, and even fights. There was no adult supervision, so we made up our own rules and settled our own differences. Not everyone would be happy with how we resolved a dispute, but I recall that most of the decisions were favorable to my teams and that my teams won most of their games. Not that I cheated, mind you; not really. All I'm saying is that I was very competitive, even then.

We played baseball at a place we called the State Field. It was a lot that was covered in cinders and rocks, with no grass, where New York State trucks and other pieces of equipment and machinery were stored. Much blood was spilled on that rough surface, including a good deal of mine. I still carry around tiny cinders from that field, visible beneath the skin on my right hand. I'll take them to my grave.

We played baseball using pieces of cardboard for bases, and balls wrapped in black electrician's tape. A new ball was a luxury, and even then it was likely to be a cheap one filled with sawdust instead of wound yarn. Or we'd use rubber-coated balls. I could make those babies curve easily. Bats were wooden back then, not aluminum, and when they broke we'd just nail them together, wrap them in tape and put them back in play. To us, they were as good as new.

We never found baseball boring. Today, many kids—and adults, too—seem to think it's a boring game, but I never did then and I don't now. We played no matter how many kids we could get together. Two-on-two and three-on-three games were common, and in fact those numbers made for very fast-paced action that we loved. Yes, we played Little League—even I did, eventually, crutches and all—but that was always secondary to our daily sandlot games.

Sadly, there's not much action on the sandlots today. For most kids, Little League is the only game in town, and many of them quickly lose interest in baseball because in the adult-supervised nine-player games there's usually a lot of standing around and waiting. Heck, I'd get bored with that, too. Baseball has many problems today, and the fact that kids no longer seem interested in playing the game without adult supervision is certainly one reason it's losing potential players and fans to other sports.

Baseball came first, but I enjoyed hockey just as much, and still do today. As kids, we played street hockey in our driveway, which eventually was illuminated by floodlights. An empty shoe polish can, weighted and wrapped in black tape, served as the puck. For goals, we cut open large cardboard boxes and weighted them down with cinderblocks placed on the flaps to keep them from being kicked around.

Most of the time, I was a goaltender, but occasionally I played forward or defense. I liked to score, so even as a goalie I'd sometimes come out of the crease on my crutches and fire a shot down the driveway for a goal. I didn't shoot very hard, but I could lift the puck off the ground, making it difficult for the other goalie to handle. At our end, I learned that I could squeeze the goalmouth tighter by pulling the cinderblocks in closer to me. When the period ended, I would be sure to move the cinderblocks back out as far as I could get them before we changed sides. You might call this cheating, but I thought of it as learning the tricks of the trade. Even then, I was thinking of how to get the upper hand.

I'd practice in goal as long as anyone wanted to take shots. Once, when several guys were practicing their shots, Dad came out to the garage to get the car, and a stray puck smacked him hard on the butt. He did a little dance and a lot of cussing, and yelled at us to knock it off.

At some point, Mom and Dad bought the apartment house next door, and that meant we had a double-wide driveway for our games.

There was just one drawback: There were shingles covering the apartment house, and when you got checked into the building during a hockey game it was like rubbing up against sandpaper. You came away from that with a painful brush burn if you weren't wearing heavy winter clothing.

Later, we graduated to mesh street hockey goals and regular hard-rubber pucks and goalie equipment. Eventually, we moved the games to frozen ponds, and much later some of us continued playing in arenas.

We had two basketball courts back then—one on our driveway, the other in our basement. In the basement, we set up a mini-court with two baskets and some seats for spectators—folding chairs, boxes and barrels. The baskets were hung so low that even I could dunk. Before the games started, I'd go around the neighborhood selling season tickets for a dime. Almost everybody bought one, but rarely did anyone show up for a game. If we had four or five spectators, that was good; 10 or more and it was standing room only.

We put the ticket money in a fund and distributed it to the players at the end of the season, with those on the championship team getting the most. I guess you could make the argument that it was our first taste of professional sports.

One year, the toy company Remco came out with a radio kit, and we bought one. I used it to do play-by-play and commentary of the basketball games from our basement—when I wasn't playing, that is—and the signal could be heard throughout the neighborhood. I never dreamed that my pretend broadcasting, like the games we played, would lead to a professional career some day, but it did. Years later, I started doing broadcasts of college and pro hockey for a local radio station during baseball's off-season.

At one time when I was a kid, I even put out a neighborhood sports newspaper. It recapped all the latest games we kids had played, complete with box scores. In my articles, I described all the scoring, added some commentary from time to time and even provided details of the fights that frequently broke out during those games. After one of the basketball games in our basement, I wrote a sidebar on the fights and headlined it: "Rumble at Games," probably figuring *that* would sell some papers. Here's an unedited excerpt from that article:

"There were 2 rumbles during the basketball game. The 1st one coming in the first half when Mick Moshier charged Dan Clark. This fumed Dan Clark who jumped Moshier. This emptied both benches and even some of the crowd came in to help hold the two players back. When this was calmed down both teams were rewarded technical foul shots.

"The second rumble broke out when Dave Clark fouled Paul Pettingill. Dave Clark flung Paul Pettingill on the floor. Pettingill then pulled Clark to the floor which started the 2nd riot. Both benches again emptied and part of the crowd emptied out of their seats to help. This resulted in 5 technical fouls for each team. This happened with just 2 seconds remaining in the game."

Well, at least I was honest about my role in that one.

I guess I was doing it all back then—organizing, playing, coaching, marketing, broadcasting and reporting.

If we didn't have a game going in those days, or if I wasn't playing one of my board or card or other make-believe games, I would always be practicing or playing in or around the house with Dan or by myself. We played football in our living room, crawling on the rug and knocking things over until Mom yelled at us. I liked to throw a tennis ball at the hard base of the couch and catch it as it bounced back. I'd throw faster and faster until one rebound would get by me and go crashing into a lamp or something else that was breakable. That would be the end of that.

I also bounced tennis balls off the garage roof and fielded them as they came down; hit rocks fungo-style with a bat (different distances meant outs, singles, home runs and so on); kicked a football out on the driveway until dark, and sometimes later; and threw a baseball against a brick wall or into a net until I got called for dinner or bed.

Looking back, I feel that I had a very vivid imagination. Radio had a lot to do with that. This was in the days when we had only a few television channels, and you didn't have your choice of a half-dozen sports events to watch on any given day or night. I got most of my sports "viewing" through the radio, and it was wonderful.

I remember going to bed with my transistor radio tucked under my pillow, or sleeping out on our oversized front porch on warm summer nights, the radio tuned to WBAL in Baltimore. The station brought all the Orioles, Clippers, Bullets and Colts games into my home. Those teams were all based in Baltimore at that time, and I was a fan of all of them. It started with the Orioles, who had a farm team in Elmira, and later spread to Baltimore's other clubs.

Listening to the announcers and the roar of the crowds, I was transported to those stadiums and arenas and I could see and smell and hear what was happening. Of course, it was all in my mind's eye, in my imagination, but that was the beauty of it. That's what made it special. As a listener, I took part in creating the scene. You just don't get that with TV. Not that I'm knocking television. I watch my share of games, and maybe more. But I still love to listen to a game on radio, especially baseball.

Imagination enabled me to look at a tennis ball and a garage roof, or a rock and a baseball bat, and devise a game, and to take that game and form teams, and to take those teams and form leagues. That wasn't just idle play, I realize now. I was developing my organizational skills and my leadership skills. And I was sharpening my playing skills at the same time.

Playing those make-believe games is the reason why, years later when I was in professional baseball, I had such good control of my pitches. That was my ticket to the pros—the fact that I could spot the ball so accurately, which I learned from throwing to spots, over and over and over again. That, and the knuckleball I began teaching myself during those throwing sessions.

I was also still developing a temper. I'll admit it: I'm a sore loser. I'm just not very good about masking my displeasure when I don't win. And maybe that's because, from an early age, losing has always made me feel that I'm not as good a person as the guy beating me. It's never been just a game. To me, it's always been personal.

When I was a kid, if one of my beloved Baltimore teams lost, I would go into a rage. When the New York Mets beat the Orioles in the 1969 World Series, I punched a hole in the bathroom wall. Another time, I threw a marble at the floor, and it bounced up and hit the TV set, chipping the screen. Frequently, I threw or punched my trusty transistor radio or stabbed it with my ever-present Bic pen.

"Dave is someone you did not want to be around if he or his team lost," Dan recalled years later. "I remember Dave used to slam his transistor radio with a pen every time his team did something bad. His radios ended up looking like pin cushions."

You might think I was nuts for acting that way, and you might be right. But that unbridled passion for winning got me where I am today. It's part of the makeup that helped me be successful at whatever I decided to do.

I firmly believe that you can't be a good loser. That doesn't mean you shouldn't treat your opponent with respect, even if he beats you; of course you should. But you have to hate losing if you're going to be a winner. I mean *hate* it.

That will to win developed strictly from within me. The kid on crutches didn't have any outside pressure to win or succeed, because nobody really was looking for much more than an honest effort. To the rest of the world, I was the ultimate underdog wherever I went, whatever I did. Nobody except my parents and me had any expectations for me, and mine always were the highest. So whatever I did, I really had nothing to lose, or so it seemed.

Of course, that all changed years later when I surprised everyone—maybe even myself—and became a professional athlete.

CHAPTER 4:

THE LITTLE LEAGUER

Pretty soon my friends started signing up for Little League, and of course I wanted to play, too. Why not? We had played against each other on the sandlots and in the streets, so this seemed like the natural progression.

But there was a problem. Not for me, but for Little League officials—the local ones in Corning and the senior ones at Little League Baseball headquarters just down Route 15 in Williamsport, Pennsylvania.

The local officials took one look at me and told my parents I couldn't play; they were afraid I'd get hurt. My parents appealed to the leaders in Williamsport, and again they were told no, it would be too dangerous for me.

I suppose people thought I'd be injured and my parents would sue them. Suing wasn't as popular back then as it is today, but I guess even I can understand, to some extent, the officials' concerns. My parents weren't the type to sue, anyway, but the folks in Little League didn't know that.

When my parents agreed to sign a waiver releasing Little League officials and their organization from any responsibility in case I got hurt, the officials gave in. This was nothing new for my parents. Earlier, when I was seven, they'd had to get a letter from my doctor and then sign a release before I could take swimming lessons at a Corning city pool—an activity that my doctor said would help strengthen my muscles.

As a 10-year-old Little Leaguer, I was assigned to Cook's TV, a minor-league team. I played first base, pitched some and spent a little time in right field—all on crutches. I remember one time in the outfield, running, diving and catching a ball. I surprised the hell out of myself, and probably a lot of other people, too.

To be honest, though, I don't have a lot of memories of Little League. I do recall being a switch-hitter because, although the Baltimore teams were always my favorites in all sports, New York Yankees slugger Mickey Mantle was one of my favorite players at the time, and he hit from both sides of the plate. I led the league in hitting after we got the okay for me to have a designated runner, somebody who would take off from the home plate area after I made contact with the ball.

And I remember both throwing and catching with my right hand, with a switchover motion similar to what people would see decades later when one-armed pitcher Jim Abbott, a lefty, made it to the major leagues. I'd throw with my right hand, the glove tucked under my left arm, then slip the glove on as I completed my pitching motion, and I was ready to field anything hit back to me. I had to make a quick switch again if I had to catch and then throw. This was particularly tough when fielding bunts or dribblers hit out in front of the plate— moving on crutches, scooping up the ball, making the switch and then throwing.

I had to field my position that way because of the leg brace that kept me from bending my left leg enough to get my left hand down to field grounders. I can clearly remember all that because I fielded the same way my whole life.

But most of the details from Little League—the games, the plays, the people—don't come back to me now as I think about those years. Maybe it was because, frankly, I always considered Little League secondary to the sandlot games. Sandlot ball was more important to my development as an athlete and a person than Little League or any other youth program. In those days, you put the Little League uniform on twice a week, then you played sandlot ball the rest of the week. Now it's just the opposite—worse, even.

I don't want to get started again on sandlot vs. Little League. There's not even cause for an argument these days. Nobody plays sandlot ball anymore. Kids wait for their coaches to tell them when to practice and when to play the games. They don't have to think about those things, and they don't have to think much during the games, either. Coaches are always there, shouting out instructions—sometimes, more than kids at that age can absorb. And parents often do the same thing. Heck, in a sandlot game, with no adult supervision and very likely fewer than nine players to a side, you're always thinking. You'd better be, anyway, and I always was.

As for my Little League years, my overall memory is of playing with and excelling against players with no physical disabilities. And that's when the seed was planted, when I realized: You can do this; you can compete with so-called able-bodied players. That's when I really started dreaming, like every other kid did, that I wanted to play in the major leagues some day. Not the Little League major leagues. The *major leagues.*

In Little League, I never did make it to the majors. I played for Cook's TV for three seasons, and then I was done.

Phil Ritz was my first coach. He didn't pamper me, and I appreciated that. I appreciate it even more today. Back then, Mr. Ritz was interviewed for a newspaper article about me, and here's what he told the reporter:

"Dave is a fine fielder and handles himself well. He is a keen student of the game and makes up for his handicap by determination and hustle. I would like to have nine boys on my team with his hustle and his ability to learn quickly.

"Dave gets the same treatment as any other member of the team. I told the other lads at the start of the season not to let up when throwing the ball to him, since Dave can handle it just as well or better than many of them."

The second season, Dad took over as manager and my brother Dan joined the team. We won the league championship but, again, the details escape me. That might surprise you if you knew me, because winning is so important to me and I don't take a championship lightly. But I don't remember that there was as much emphasis on winning back then as there is today, even in Little League, so maybe it's just that we all pretty much took it in stride.

Looking back on my Little League experience, I can't help but think how fortunate I was to grow up in a time and place where I was given the opportunity to succeed at that age and at that level and to begin to develop my skills. Sure, there was some opposition at first, but everything got settled. If I had been living somewhere else—some big city, let's say—I probably would have been channeled into a special school for kids with disabilities. In Corning, I was mainstreamed before mainstreaming was a word that applied to a classroom. And in another place and time, I probably wouldn't have gotten the chance to prove myself in baseball against kids without disabilities, and to win their acceptance. I never would have felt the need to excel.

And that was so important to me. I can remember, as a kid, having strong feelings of being disabled. I wanted so much to fit in. I didn't want anybody to feel sorry for me or look at me differently. I'm pretty sure I wouldn't have approved if somebody had steered me toward a league for kids with disabilities. That might be okay for some, but it would have been disastrous for me.

Today, though, I'd be placed on a Challenger team. Challenger is Little League's division for children with physical and mental disabilities. For many children today—kids who truly would have no other opportunity to play—Challenger is a great thing, believe me. I think it's wonderful that people are looking out for the interests of those kids. So I don't want what I'm going to write next to be interpreted as anything negative against that league and the people who give so generously of their time to make it succeed.

But the simple truth is this: If I had been placed on a Challenger team, it would have been the beginning and the end of my life in organized sports. I would have played however many years they allowed, turned in my uniform and disappeared. I wouldn't have been allowed to play with a glove on my right hand. I wouldn't have been challenged mentally or physically, as I was challenged every day in my own situation. It sounds funny, maybe, but for me the Challenger Division would have been no challenge at all.

Playing baseball at an early age helped me become very analytical. And that was so important, because my brain got me further than anything else. It's like that doctor told my mother when he first informed her I had polio: "If he can just use his mind."

I was always analyzing, even then—figuring out my strengths and limitations, for example. That was true in all the sports I played.

In baseball, I knew I had no speed, no quickness, and I couldn't throw hard. But I had become a good fielder, even as a kid, and I had developed pinpoint control as a pitcher from all that throwing at targets. So I focused on pitching and playing first base, where you don't have to move around as much as most other positions but where you have to be good with the glove. Eventually—just after Little League, in fact—I began to teach myself how to throw the knuckleball that would become my "out" pitch as a professional player.

If I had been placed on a "special" team of some sort at that time, I wonder what my analysis of the situation would have been. Not promising, I'm sure. There's no way I could have developed as an athlete, and I don't even want to think about the way my life might have turned out in that case. I'm not saying it would have been tragic, but certainly it wouldn't have taken me where I've gone or allowed me to do what I've done.

Tragic would be if, with all those good intentions, we inadvertently deny some other young boy or girl the same shot at life that I had. It would be rare, certainly. But you know, there just might be another Dave Clark out there.

We need to be very careful not to stereotype people or establish limits for them before giving them an opportunity. I like the old adage, "Don't judge a book by its cover." No one knows what's inside without taking the time to open a book and read—or, in the case of an individual, to watch and listen.

Today, as a baseball scout, that's perhaps the most difficult thing for me do—to read what's inside a player. What's in his heart? Does he have the desire, the drive, to become the best player he can possibly be? Will he overcome the obstacles he must surely face? The answers to these questions are probably more important in the long run than a player's sheer physical ability. Ability alone won't get him were he wants to go.

Chapter 5:

The Knuckler

In the early 1960s, at about the time I got into Little League, my dad started taking me to minor-league baseball games at Dunn Field in Elmira. The team, which had several different affiliations and played in several different leagues over the years, was a Baltimore Orioles farm team in the Class AA Eastern League at the time.

By then I was so independent that I didn't want to accept anything from anybody, including my parents. At the ballgames, for example, I wanted to buy my own ticket. I had saved my money, and I wanted to pay my own way. My parents didn't want me to pay, but they went along with my wishes because I was so adamant about it. But it would drive me crazy if some friend was with us at a game or someplace else and Mom or Dad bought a ticket or a treat for him. It wasn't that I felt cheated. It's just that I had developed the attitude that we shouldn't allow ourselves, even at that age, to be so dependent on others.

Those baseball games in Elmira really fired my imagination—and not just the games themselves, but the whole experience. I remember getting there early one time and being out in the parking lot when the bus carrying the visiting team came rolling in. The Elmira Pioneers were playing the Phillies from Reading, Pennsylvania. I can still see the bus with its logo for the Red Lion Bus Company, and wondering about the trip that had brought it to us.

(Corning also had a minor-league team, the Royals, a short-season Class A affiliate of the Kansas City Royals, in the New York-Penn League. That team lasted just two seasons, 1967 and '68. Later, Elmira joined that league, and still later the city lost its affiliation and moved to an independent league. As of this writing, Elmira no longer has a pro team but instead is fielding a summer college-league club.)

A ballplayer's life on the road always seemed so glamorous to me—getting out on the open highway, traveling to new and different places, and having somebody else do all the driving. Traveling by rail was even better, at least in my mind. To me, that was one of the things that life as a professional baseball player could give you—free travel to destinations only a child's mind could imagine. Much later, I found out it isn't so glamorous at all.

After Little League, I didn't play organized baseball for a few years. Then I joined the Southern Zone League, for players of high school age and older. After pitching and playing first base and occasionally the outfielder in Little League, I now focused on pitching. My analytical brain had figured it out: You're down to your last shot, buddy.

I was prepared, though. During that down time after Little League, I had developed what would become my ticket to the minors, and nearly to the majors: the knuckleball. It happened out of necessity. I had what is known as a Kleenex fastball—it couldn't break tissue paper. At best, I got it up there at seventy-nine miles an hour.

By experimentation, I learned to throw the knuckler, a pitch that doesn't rely on speed and, in fact, can't be thrown fast because of the way it's gripped—with the fingernails, actually, and not the knuckles. I tried different grips on different parts of the ball, and different deliveries using each grip. I'd throw against a brick wall endlessly. Finally, I settled on a grip and release and arm angle that worked best for me.

I gripped the ball with the fingernails of four fingers, with my ring and middle fingers digging into the seams on the narrow part of the stitching. I'd throw in an easy, effortless motion with a three-quarter-arm delivery and a locked wrist. That last part is very important. To get the ball to flutter and dip and float around as it approaches the plate, you can't push it away with the fingers. The ball must simply be released, with the arm motion propelling it.

The knuckleball isn't taught much anymore because in today's game it's all about speed and power. Many people consider the knuckler to be a wimpy pitch. But just try to hit it. You can't—not if it's a good one, and I had a good one. Even major-league hitters, when they get the rare experience of seeing a knuckleball, have great difficulty with it. And I've always thought pitching was about getting hitters out, anyway you can.

All I know is the knuckleball was the catalyst for my career. It took me three years to master it, and when I was done I didn't need a fastball anymore. I threw the knuckler at a speed in the mid-fifties, and for that pitch it was all I needed.

I played in the Southern Zone League during my four years of high school. (I didn't go out for the high school team.) I was on a club called the Corning Yankways, a nickname that somebody arrived at by combining Yankees and Fenway Park, the name of Boston's great old ballpark. It was an unlikely combination, the Yanks and Red Sox being the fierce rivals they are, but we were a pretty good team.

During those years, I started writing to major-league baseball clubs, asking for a tryout. In each letter, I explained my situation, all of it, letting them know where I was coming from but also making sure they knew where I hoped to go. Now that I sit here thinking about it, I'm struck by how absurd that was. Imagine me thinking I was good enough to have some big-league organization even give me a look. But with the innocence of youth, and maybe a little cockiness, I did it.

With my trusty Bic pen, I wrote twenty-four separate hand-written letters, one to each major-league general manager. Only three of them even bothered to respond—Gabe Paul in Cleveland, Lew Matlin in Detroit and Frank Cashen with my beloved Baltimore Orioles.

Cashen invited me to Baltimore. I met him at Memorial Stadium, and he let me try out. Looking back, I think it was just a nice gesture on his part. But to me, it was huge. I was thrilled. And you know, I think I surprised even Cashen. In any case, he gave me a job—not as a player, but as an associate scout.

Now I was in professional baseball, at least in a small way. I still believed I could play there, and I was determined to prove it eventually. But I've always looked at the glass as being half full, so I was excited just to be a part of that wonderful world that I had dreamed of for so long. I was proud to be a scout, and I enjoyed my working relationship with John Stokoe, the East Coast Regional Scouting Supervisor for the Orioles. I still occasionally see John today.

I've continued scouting, on and off, for much of my adult life. I've worked for the New York Yankees, Chicago White Sox, Florida Marlins, Atlanta Braves and San Diego Padres, in addition to the Orioles.

While I was thrilled to get my first paying job in baseball, not everybody in the family shared my excitement. My grandfather—my Mom's dad, Jim Strawser—told me I should go get a job at what was then Corning Glass Works. He worked there, most of my mom's family worked there, and even Mom herself had worked there. It was a good, solid company, a Fortune 500 company, just as it is today under its new name, Corning Incorporated. (My dad's side of the family all worked for Ingersoll-Rand, a fine company, too, and, like Corning Incorporated, a solid member of the community.)

I didn't want to disappoint my grandfather or anyone else, but I could never see myself as a factory worker or an office worker, so I stayed the course. I had my dream and I was determined to see it become a reality.

My chance to play pro baseball came a few months after my meeting with Frank Cashen. I was invited to the Art Gaines Baseball School in Missouri. It was run by Gaines, a former Pittsburgh Pirate who was then a scout for the Pirates and who was looking for players for the Hunnewell Gators, an independent team in Missouri with ties to the Pirates.

I was lucky to survive the first day of camp. My first time at bat, in a bunting drill for pitchers, I squared around and promptly fouled the first pitch straight back into my right eye. My eye swelled up like an orange, and I remember thinking: *Well, this was nice while it lasted.*

Gaines was another man who refused to give me special treatment. Later in that camp, I tore the skin under my arm with one of my crutches while running sprints in the outfield. It was on the sixteenth of twenty sprints. Gaines could have pulled me aside, got me some medical attention, and let me skip the rest of the drill. But, thankfully, he didn't. He made me finish, and I did.

A couple of years later, I attended another camp, the Fort Lauderdale Baseball Camp run by Fred Ferreira, who was a scout for the Philadelphia Phillies. Another scout, Danny Pfister, a former pitcher for the Oakland A's, watched me work out at Fred's camp and wrote in his report:

"If David's physical ability matched his desire and determination to be a ballplayer, he would be a superstar in the big leagues. Has shown amazing ability to hit and field and compete with players his age. My feelings about this young man are the highest of any person I have ever been associated with in baseball. He will succeed."

I'm flattered, of course. And I agree with his assessment that if my physical ability had indeed matched my desire and determination, there would have been no stopping me. But I've always felt that it was only because of my physical limitations that my desire and determination were so strong. If I'd been just another so-called able-bodied kid, I doubt I'd have had the need to succeed that has driven me all my life.

After I left for the Art Gaines camp in Missouri, my mom wrote to Gaines, asking him to please let me down easy when the time came. I didn't know about it—not then, and not until much, much later. Mom even sent Gaines a return envelope, addressed to a neighbor's house so I wouldn't see his reply.

It wasn't necessary. I made the cut.

Twenty-five years later, Mom reluctantly told me about her letter. Through tears, she said to me, "How could I have doubted you?"

Chapter 6:

Turning Point

Something happened during my teen years that could have changed the course of my life but, thankfully, didn't.

Looking back, I see it as every bit as significant as Mr. Schnetzler's second-grade gym class. If either event hadn't happened just as it did, I wouldn't be telling you about my career in sports. I never would have made it to the Art Gaines baseball camp or gotten a chance from anyone else to play pro ball. In fact, I probably never would have competed in any sport again.

Here's what happened:

When I was sixteen, my doctors in Elmira suggested that I see a specialist because of their concerns about the severe curvature of my spine. I guess it had to happen sooner or later. My back is bad; I know it is. From time to time over the years, I've seen X-rays, and they are scary.

My parents agreed to take me to the specialist, and so one day they drove me to Strong Memorial Hospital in Rochester, New York, where eventually I was led into an examining room where I was greeted by a tall, distinguished-looking gentleman whom I immediately disliked. From the moment we first met, I viewed him as my enemy.

The doctor, whose name I can't recall, had a very persuasive manner about him. He obviously knew what he was talking about, and as I sat listening to him I sensed that my parents were hanging on his every word. For someone who had just met me, he seemed certain he knew what was best for me, judging strictly from the X-rays he had studied and from his experience with cases like mine. When he got down to specifics and recommended that I have metal rods inserted into my back to hold my spine in place, I remember feeling fear and anger and thinking, *"This guy is going to talk my parents into doing this!"*

"You won't have as much mobility in your back," the doctor told me, meaning with the rods. "You'll have to bend from your hips."

"What about going up steps?" I asked.

"You'll have to re-learn that."

Would I have to re-learn how to pitch, too? How to hit? I wanted to ask those questions, but I didn't. I thought I knew the answers.

No matter how big the odds, I've always been able to look past my limitations and see myself as a professional baseball player. But this? With rods supporting my back, preventing me from bending, making me look like some Munster on the mound? I tried to think of myself throwing a ball and visualized somebody looking like one of those old Iron Mike pitching machines.

"But I want to play baseball," I said at one point. "Professional baseball."

That must have sounded pretty far-fetched, at least if you were listening. But the doctor didn't even seem to hear me. He certainly never considered what I was saying. He brushed off the comment as if I had said I hoped to flap my arms and fly one day, and he went back to making a case for this procedure he was proposing.

The specialist told me what the doctors in Elmira had already said—that with rods to support my spine I could be six feet tall, or taller. That seemed reasonable, I thought. My dad was five-nine, my brother Doug was six feet and Dan was six-two, so it figured that I could probably be better than average height. And, being five-two, that part had some appeal. (Later, teams often listed me at five-three, but that was being generous.) As far as I was concerned, though, the rods would only make me taller—they wouldn't allow me to do what I wanted to do with my life.

My parents listening intently to everything the specialist said and didn't say much in return, and I wasn't sure how to take that. They considered everything and then told the doctor we would wait. If the procedure had to be done later, it would be done later, they said. For now, we would all just live with it.

Dad says: "We prayed about it later. We decided that we were going to let the Lord take care of whatever was going to be done. Dave had enough of a burden on him without having that, too."

I was so happy, I could have hugged them both right there. When they gave the doctor their decision, I felt a tremendous sense of relief.

My parents knew I had a dream and, as crazy as it must have seemed to most people, they wanted me to have a shot at it. They knew the polio had already severely limited what I could do. And they knew that doing what this doctor suggested would kill my dream. It would help me in one way but would end my chances of playing baseball. They didn't like the trade-off, and neither did I.

"You'll regret it if you don't do this," the doctor persisted. "You will regret it."

Looking at me sternly, he said: "You'll have back problems all your life. And when you finally do decide to do this, it will be a more difficult procedure the older you are."

Instead of giving in, I counter-attacked, going for more. I told the doc I wanted to remove the brace from my right leg. Ever since I was old enough to walk, I had worn braces on both legs. They ran all the way up the legs to my hips, where a belt was wrapped around my body, connecting the braces at my waist. The belt was tied front and back with shoelaces.

"Absolutely not," he told me. "I would strongly recommend against it."

It's something I had been thinking about doing, and this just seemed like the right time to bring it up. With the two braces, I'd been able to play baseball well enough in the streets as a kid and in organized programs like Little League and the Southern Zone League. But I had begun to realize that if I wanted to take that next step to pro ball—and I did, more than anything—then I needed to give myself a little edge. I could get the edge, add some mobility, by freeing up my right leg. Yeah, that's what I would do.

On the way back from Rochester that day, I told my parents I was going to remove the brace, no matter what the doctor said. They didn't argue. If I thought it was something I should do, they said, then, yes, do it. When we got home, I went into the house, undid the right brace and pulled it off. I've never worn it since.

I recall that day and can't help but feel that it was a major turning point in my life and my career. My parents rejected back surgery, and I removed the brace from my right leg—again, with my parents' blessing.

If I could talk to the parents of children with disabilities, I'd ask them to at least consider what my parents did for me that day. The easy way out would have been to take the advice of a specialist. This man knew medicine, and from his perspective he was absolutely right: Surgery would have been the best thing for me. But he didn't know *me*, and my parents did.

Parents need to consider how a medical procedure—or any other life-changing development—will affect their children's future. Give your kids every opportunity to improve their physical or psychological conditions, but consider their hopes and dreams, too.

I'm over fifty years old now, and I've never had surgery on my back. But my back is still a mess, and I know it. Every time a doctor looks at my back for the first time, it's the same story.

"What medication are you taking?" they'll typically ask.

"For what?" I'll say.

"Your back. You must be in terrible pain."

"I'm not in any pain."

And they can't believe it. The only way they can explain it is to say the daily exercise routine I've followed religiously over the years must have strengthened the muscles in my back enough that they supported my spine.

I could still have the back surgery today, but as the specialist in Rochester warned me, it would be a much riskier procedure because of my age. Of course, science and technology have advanced greatly from when I was a teenager. But I don't have the muscle today that I had when I was younger and more active. Besides, I'm now feeling the effects of post-polio syndrome, so I don't know how my body would react to surgery.

I've never given much thought to what it would have been like to have metal rods in my back. But in thinking about it now, I have to wonder if at some point those rods don't wear out. Would the rods have created new problems for me over time, maybe given me more pain? Would I have needed follow-up surgery? I just don't know.

What I do know is that I never would have played baseball or hockey again. I wouldn't have coached or managed or scouted in professional baseball. I wouldn't have gone to Sweden, met my future wife, or fathered the beautiful daughter we have today. I wouldn't have heard the roar of the crowd—the cheers and, yes, occasionally the boos.

What scares me is that I might have become the kind of person who doesn't take chances, who doesn't push the envelope, who doesn't ignore the odds. I might have become a different person altogether.

If my parents hadn't rejected back surgery, if I hadn't gone home and taken off the right leg brace, I might have gone on to become an accountant with a nice big desk and a corner office and maybe even a secretary. I don't mean to knock accountants or accounting—or any other profession or way of life. But those jobs just aren't for me. Yet if things had been different, that's where I might be today—hard at work in an office somewhere, sitting tall and straight behind my desk, dressed in a nice expensive suit, and bored to death. Hating it.

Chapter 7:

Call Me Coach

Hockey, not baseball, is now my favorite sport to watch.

Maybe that's partly because baseball became my job. It's a job I've always loved, but I don't think you can ever enjoy what you do as an occupation the way you can something you do just because you love it. Anyway, if I hadn't had any physical limitations, I'd have concentrated on playing hockey rather than baseball.

In hockey, I was limited to playing goalie, the position I played in those street games back home. Selecting that position didn't require any effort from my analytical mind. I couldn't skate, so forward and defense were out. Even goalie was a stretch, but I made it work. Fortunately, I liked it, and I was pretty good at it, too.

After graduating from Corning East High School in 1970, I entered Corning Community College, a two-year school up on Spencer Hill in Corning, and played for a club hockey team. In 1976, I helped organize an adult league, the Southern Tier Hockey Association. We had teams in Elmira, Horseheads, Elmira Heights, Bath and Penn Yan, in addition to Corning. I played for Harvard Mutual of Corning, which was sponsored by a local insurance agency and which later became the Totem Taxi Indians, sponsored by a cab company.

Every year, we played in a benefit tournament called the Crystal City Classic Cup, which drew teams from all over New York State to

Corning. The tournament was played in February or March, in the Nasser Civic Center, which is an outdoor rink with only a few seats. You can imagine how cold it was, yet we packed the place, with fans standing three and four deep along the boards.

The first year, Harvard Mutual and a team called Cullen's Sporting Goods played in the finals, a best-of-five series. We won in four games, taking the deciding game 5–2. My brother Dan had one goal for us in that game. I made 15 saves and was fortunate enough to be named the first star. If you don't know hockey, that's like being the game's MVP.

I can still hear them announcing my name: Dave "Chico" Clark. That's what they called me back then—Chico—because Glenn "Chico" Resch was the goaltender for the Stanley Cup champion New York Islanders at the time.

The next year, we played Penn Yan in the finals, this time as Totem Taxi. We were up two games to one with a 5–4 lead and about two minutes left to play in Game 4 when I was involved in one of the biggest plays of my life.

This player for Penn Yan, a guy named Coley King, stole the puck and came at me on a breakaway. He was the most feared player in the league, the last guy you'd want to see heading your way with no defender in sight. And there he was. I set myself and waited as King came charging in.

He turned me around like a pretzel. He made a move and my legs went one way, my stick went another, and I twisted completely around so that I was facing the net, my glove hand stretched out in desperation across the crease. Somehow, the puck wound up in my glove and stuck there. Incredibly, unbelievably, I had made the save.

My teammates went nuts, piling on me and screaming in my ear. King slammed his stick to the ice in frustration, shattering it. I looked in my glove, just to be sure, and saw the puck nestled there.

We had won the tournament.

Later, I was named to the all-tournament team. It's an honor I still treasure.

Hockey wasn't all spectacular saves and honors, though. It's a rough, tough sport, and it can take a physical toll.

Twice I was hit in the face so hard by a flying puck, the old flat mask I used to wear in those days was split and I was left bloodied.

The first time was in a game against the Cornell University junior varsity at Cornell's Lynah Rink. I faced an incredible seventy-nine shots in that one—about twice what a National Hockey League goalie might see on a busy night—and we lost 14–2. To add injury to insult, I caught one between the eyes late in the game, and the shot cracked my mask down the middle and ripped my skin open. It took four stitches to sew me up.

My brother Dan was responsible for the other, more serious, injury. That happened in warm-ups before a Southern Tier Hockey Association game at the Murray Athletic Center, the Elmira College rink. Usually if you're taking a slap shot in warm-ups, you go low. But for some reason, Dan, who had a wicked slap shot, brought the puck in close this time, took aim and let loose up high.

I watched him with growing concern as he skated in, thinking, *Come on, Dan, what is this? … What IS this? … What the …*

WHACK!

The puck caught me high on the mask, shattering the plastic and bloodying my face. For just a moment, I saw stars. Then I fell backward and lay motionless as blood poured from the deep gash on my face, turning the ice red all around me—or so I was told later. The next thing I knew, I was at the hospital.

When I came to, I was lying on my back in the emergency room, a doctor hovering over me, stitching up my forehead. Suddenly there was a call for the doctor over the intercom, and he walked out and left me there. Turns out some guy was having a heart attack—a more serious problem, even, than mine. After a while, the doc came back and finished with me—twelve or fifteen stitches in all.

Hey, thanks, Dan.

I had some great times in net, though. And I was feisty—always wanting to mix it up, pushing guys out of the way, tapping defensemen in the back of the knee with my stick if they got too close. I was very protective of my space.

But there's only so far you can go as a goalie who can't skate. After those few years, my hockey playing career was over. Years later, I would return to the sport, this time as a radio broadcaster, mostly for Elmira College's fine Division III men's hockey team.

After graduating from Corning Community College in 1972 with a degree in humanities and social sciences, I attended Ithaca College. In retrospect, that was ironic—going back to the city where, as an infant, I made some of my earliest strides, even learning to walk with crutches. And then, many years later, Ithaca College honored me with a place in its Athletic Hall of Fame. Go figure.

Some officials at Ithaca College balked at my selecting Physical Education as my major. They told me I was unemployable in that field, and they threatened to shut off the federal aid I was receiving because of my disability. But I argued to keep my major, and I won. I got my bachelor's degree there in 1974.

My goal, if I hadn't gone into professional baseball, was to become a teacher and a coach. Toward that end, I did my student teaching at schools in Ithaca and Corning.

While I was at Ithaca College, I was engaged to a girl named Shirley Ripley, who was a student at Corning Community College. One day, Shirley saw a bulletin-board notice announcing that Corning was going to start a baseball program, something it hadn't had until then, and that it was looking for a coach. Shirley knew I loved baseball and that I played on a club team at Ithaca, so she told me about the notice. I applied for the job as head coach and was hired.

As Corning coach, I delivered a lot of firsts: first winning season, first trip south, first regional playoffs. We played eight games that first season. The Ithaca College junior varsity beat us 5–4 in our opener, scoring three runs in the ninth inning. We won our last game, beating the Cornell University jayvees 4–3 in the second game of a doubleheader.

Denis Sweeney of Corning was one of my players. My brother Dan was another. Years later, in 2002 and 2003, Denis became my agent as I began building my public speaking career. Here's how Denis later remembered his first meeting with me when he went out for the Corning baseball team:

"When I entered the locker room, I saw a short man on crutches with a clipboard and blue Bic pen in hand. My first thoughts were, who is this guy, and how is he involved with the baseball team? As I approached him, he stuck out his right hand to me and said, 'Hi, I'm Dave Clark, the baseball coach.' As he was shaking my hand—or, more appropriately, crushing it with his strength—I became blinded to Dave's crutches. From that second on, I never ever considered him a disabled person. He ran, pitched and hit with us in practice like everyone else. From my observations of Dave Clark as coach, the word 'can't' never appeared in his vocabulary or was uttered from his lips."

The Red Barons played spring and fall seasons, which worked out perfectly for me. I was able to continue with my baseball playing career during summers and also coach the college team.

My next year at CCC, they gave me a second job. In addition to the baseball coach, I was now the college's first physical activities director. It was a new position created to provide experiences and challenges for students with physical limitations.

As happy as I was to get the position, I wasn't at all sure it was right for me. Frankly, I went into the job feeling a bit uncomfortable.

The reason might surprise you. It's simply this: I had never before associated with people with physical disabilities. As I've said, I was mainstreamed in school, so that I was always in classes where all the other children were so-called able-bodied boys and girls. And when I played sports, which was a large part of my life, I competed against all the other kids, generally following all the same rules and using all the same equipment they did—except, of course, for my crutches; none of them had crutches. Other than that, I considered us all to be the same.

As a result, I didn't relate to the students who were assigned to me, these young people with various physical limitations. I didn't know what to do with them, where to take them, how to help them. For the first week on my new job, I sat there staring at the four walls of my office, waiting for inspiration.

Finally, it hit me that everybody needs to exercise, so I set up an exercise class. We did aerobics, strength drills and things like that. Then I gave the students bowling lessons and took them bowling. Next, we went on trips to see hockey games in Binghamton, which had an American Hockey League team. We went boating, fishing and camping. And we had social get-togethers.

I just made it up as I went along. But I went too far.

Figuring that if we could drive an hour or ninety minutes to Binghamton to watch hockey, we could take a little longer trip, say to Washington, D.C. One day an article appeared in The Leader, the Corning newspaper, saying that I had scheduled a weekend getaway— three days and two nights—to the Baltimore-Washington area for disabled people who liked hockey. I mean *really* liked hockey. We were to see four games in those three days. Today, that seems like a lot, even for me. Well, the college administrators felt the same way. My boss told me to can the trips, and that was the end of that idea.

The bowling went over well, though. I started the Corning Community College Disabled Persons Bowling League at Crystal Lanes in Corning, where they let us bowl for free. We bowled on Sundays and opened the competition to anyone with a disability, not just students. We even had one division for people in wheelchairs.

I bowled in the league, too. A friend named Tom Fletcher and I were regular-season champions that first year.

While at Corning Community College, I helped establish Greenhouse, one of the first group homes in our area. It was for people with mental and physical disabilities. The home remains in operation today, under a new name: Accessories to Independence and Mobility (AIM).

I'm grateful for the opportunity the job at the college gave me to meet other people with disabilities and to interact with them, even if that didn't come easy at first. Between that job and Greenhouse and the camps for the disabled that came later, I'm glad I was able to help so many people in my own small way. I wish for each of them, and for those who follow them, the same success and happiness I've found in my life.

CHAPTER 8:

PROVING MYSELF

Now I was in uncharted waters.

After Art Gaines signed me in 1971 and I joined the team in Hunnewell, Missouri, I quickly discovered that professional baseball was a whole new game.

Technically, the Hunnewell Gators were semi-pro, not pro. But semi-pro in those days wasn't what it is today. These days, when you hear the term you think of a loosely organized collection of weekend pick-up games. In those days, it was something more closely related to the independent leagues they have now. Semi-pros were paid; we had contracts with our teams. We considered ourselves professionals, no matter what the terminology.

And in the pros, you find it's not just fun and games anymore. When I got to Hunnewell, I quickly discovered the street games, the Little League, the teen league, college—that was all behind me, way behind me. I was eighteen years old now, and a pro.

Professional players work hard every day, trying to make a living, looking to impress someone, hoping—as I was—to move up the ladder and one day, maybe, get a shot at the big show.

They will do anything at that level to beat you—and, really, you can't expect anything less. Heck, I had the same attitude, plus a new level of confidence now that I'd been signed. If somebody else thought I could play at that level—somebody whose job it was to evaluate prospects every day—how could I think any less of myself? Well, I didn't. But now I would be pitching to guys who would take any edge you gave them and turn it against you. If they saw a pitcher out on the mound who needed crutches to get around, for example, you're damn right they'd drop down a bunt for an easy base hit.

That's how it went at Hunnewell, and later at all the other stops during my pro career. There were always a few hitters who thought they could take advantage of the situation by laying one down—certainly more than other pitchers faced. And so we had to adjust—the Gaters, and later the other teams I played for.

Here's what we'd do: The third baseman and first baseman would pinch in at the corners, and the catcher would be set to spring out of his squat position as the bunt came off the bat. The second baseman would be ready to cover first, and if there was a runner at first the shortstop would hustle to the bag at second in case we tried for the force—or he might have to cover third if there was a runner at second.

We'd work it out so the catcher would make the play on balls hit halfway to the mound, and I'd take care of anything beyond that. But I could help only on balls hit straight to me. Anything to either side was the responsibility of the third baseman or first baseman.

Basically, we were playing a sacrifice bunt defense, regardless of the situation. And with the men at the corners playing shallower than usual, and with the middle infielders often "cheating" to the bag they'd have to cover, we sometimes gave up hits on ground balls that otherwise would have been easy outs. It's the price we had to pay.

As for the batters who insisted on bunting against me anyway, well, some of them paid a price, too. As I've said, I threw mostly knuckleballs, with an occasional slow curve and a seventy-nine-mile-an-hour fastball mixed in. That's not fast for the pros, but even a ball thrown at seventy-nine will hurt if it hits you, and I had no problem plunking somebody if I thought he deserved it. Of course, that usually meant I had to pay the price, too. There was no designated hitter in those days—and wouldn't be for two more years, until 1973—so I had to take my turn at bat.

I remember one game when a DH would have saved me a headache—literally—but would have kept me from learning a valuable lesson.

This happened when I was with Hunnewell, in a game at Hannibal, Missouri. It was in the late innings, and I was pitching with two outs and the other team's pitcher at second base. He took off at the crack of the bat when the next batter hit one to left-center, and I was slow getting to the line on my way to back up the plate. This other pitcher came charging around third base, heading for home, just as I crossed the line. He raced past, just behind me, and scored the go-ahead run.

I was mad at myself, and frustrated, having just given up the lead run with two outs. Instead of throwing my knuckler, I had hung a curve ball. And, on top of that, I had let their pitcher score the run that gave him the lead.

Over my shoulder, I swore at the pitcher as he ran past me. Big mistake.

I led off the next inning, and I knew what to expect. Back then it was an accepted part of baseball: You did something like that and you paid for it. I shot my mouth off, and I knew I'd get hit. Still, I didn't like the idea. But I dug in the batter's box, again supported by crutches, and I waited.

The first pitch buzzed under my chin, and I spun away from it and turned to their catcher—who happened to have been traded away from our team just a couple of weeks before—and I said, "Bill, I hope that one just got away." He assured me it had.

Well, it hadn't. The next pitch hit me in the helmet, right on the left flap at my temple, and I went down in a heap.

When I came to, sprawled out on the dirt at the plate, I opened my eyes and saw a brawl going on out on the field. Players on both sides were pushing, shoving and punching each other. It was one of the prettiest sights I've ever seen. I just smiled to myself and thought: *My guys are behind me.*

They sent in a pinch-runner for me, and he scored as we took the lead for good that inning. I got credit for the win.

Looking back, I'm pretty sure that if that incident had happened during the first few weeks of the season, the guys would have sat on the bench and waited for me to wake up. But by this time I had proved myself, I had showed that I belonged. It made all the difference.

It was that way with every team. I had to prove myself over and over again. There was about a two-week period of adjustment everywhere I played, during which I had to show the other players that I was one of them—and as good as them—and not just a novelty act. I had to earn their acceptance. That was okay, though. It was just part of my job. Heck, I'd always had to prove myself, everywhere and in everything I did. Why should this be any different?

Wherever I played, I was always the first guy on the field, stretching and running sprints, and the last guy out of the weight room if there was one. I needed to work harder than the other players to stay where I was, and I did. I put in the time, and they saw that. Eventually, they all came to accept me. Well, almost all.

There was this one guy, whose name I can't remember—not that I really want to. I'll never forget what he did to me, though, and what I did to him.

This was 1977, and I was trying out for the Beeville (Texas) Bees in the old Class A Gulf States League. We were playing a night game in Beeville, and I came on in relief in the seventh inning with the score tied 3–3, the bases loaded and two outs.

I got my first batter to hit a lazy fly ball to left field. It was a routine play, what we call a can of corn, a floater with a lot of hang time. With two outs, the runners were going, but we were out of the inning. Having done my job, I gave the ball a glance as it drifted into left and then began walking off the mound.

Then the ball dropped. The left fielder made no real attempt to catch it, never even got a glove on it. He just jogged over towards the ball and then took his time picking it up after it had finished rolling. By the time he tossed it back to the infield, all three runners had scored and the hitter was on second base.

I was stunned. And I was livid. When I heard the crowd's reaction as the ball dropped, I stopped in my tracks, halfway to the dugout, and just glared at our left fielder. It was clear to everybody in the ballpark that he'd let the ball drop on purpose. And what was his purpose? To make me look bad.

I went back to the mound, grumbling to myself, almost too mad to throw straight. But I did throw straight, and the next batter made an out and the inning was over.

We trotted into the dugout, and the left fielder sat down at the end of the bench closest to the outfield. I went in, took a sip from the water fountain at the other end of the dugout, walked the entire length of the bench and then sprang at the guy. I grabbed him by the throat and started choking him. He was pretty big, and he could have crushed me, but he'd have paid for it. He'd have been hurt.

I swore at him and screamed in his face, "You tanked it!"

He cursed back at me but didn't deny it. He knew what he'd done.

Our teammates pulled us apart then. The left fielder and I never discussed the incident again and, in fact, never talked to each other after that. And I never pitched for the Bees again. A couple of days later I was cut.

I don't think that incident had anything to do with my release. Our manager, Bill Bryk, called me into his office and told me the Phillies organization was sending down another pitcher. Beeville had a working relationship with Philadelphia, and so it was a case of the Bees having to take this pitcher and let someone go. That someone was me.

In all my years in baseball, I had only one other run-in with a player who tried to make me look bad just because he didn't want to play with somebody on crutches. That happened in Sweden, and that time we ended up throwing punches.

There was another time when a fan got on me and I retaliated and nearly caused a riot at a ballpark in Jefferson City, Missouri. It was 1975, and I was pitching for the Indianapolis Clowns, a longtime barnstorming team that was then in the Class A Mississippi Valley League. (Barnstorming teams, once fairly common, traveled the country, going from town to town, playing a local team and then moving on.) In this particular game, I came out of the bullpen in the sixth or seventh inning with the score tied, two outs and the bases full. The stands were full, too, with four thousand or five thousand fans packed into the ballpark.

I took my eight warm-up pitches, the umpire dusted off home plate, and I got set on the mound. Then, from behind home plate, this leather-lung yelled, "All right, let's knock the crippled bastard out of there!"

I stepped back off the rubber and steamed for a bit. There are lots of things fans can say to get under an opposing player's skin, but I've never liked the personal attacks—against me or anyone else. I've sometimes wondered what Jackie Robinson must have gone through, for example, as the first black player in the major leagues. It must have been awful. How could the man concentrate? And yet he did, and was a great player.

Not that I compare myself to Jackie in any way, but I guess I can empathize a little. I no more chose to have polio than Robinson chose the color of his skin—and I'm not saying he would have changed it if he could. We're all born with certain physical characteristics, and for somebody to attack us for that is beyond stupid. There are stupid people, though, so what can you do?

Anyway, I listened to this jerk behind home plate and let him get to me. After I fumed for a while, I stuck the ball in my glove and, in the same motion, threw the guy the finger, thinking somehow the gesture was blocked from view of the other fans. It wasn't.

The stands erupted. Fans booed and yelled out at me, and showered the field with beer. I was lucky they didn't jump the fence and come out after me.

My manager, Bill Heward, did come out. He walked from the dugout to talk to me—to calm me down, and the fans, too, and to teach me a lesson.

Bill was a good manager. He was a master at keeping his players happy, using his entire roster throughout the season so that everybody got a chance to play and to stay sharp. I liked him and respected his opinion, even if I didn't always agree with it.

Bill was not happy when he reached the mound. He turned his back to the crowd and got in my face.

"Don't ever let me see you do that again," he said.

"But ..."

"No. You ever put on a display like that again, and you'll be on the next Greyhound home. You've got to learn to deal with these knuckleheads, and you better start now. If you can't pitch with some idiot yelling at you from the stands, then you can't pitch in this league."

Bill left, and I stood at the mound by myself for a while, listening to the crowd giving it to me even louder now. And I decided Bill was right. There *were* knuckleheads out there, and I would have to learn to deal with them and with situations like that. And I had to start now.

I got out of the inning, but I don't remember how. We scored some runs and won, and again I got credit for the victory.

Not all the knuckleheads I came across were fans or lazy outfielders. Some were in responsible positions where they could influence the thinking of others. One I encountered was a sportswriter in Kearney, Nebraska.

I was still with the Clowns, and this was still 1975. The whole thing started in another tie game, 4–4 this time in the bottom of the ninth, bases loaded with one out when I was brought in from the bullpen. I got the first batter to pop to short. One out to go.

Our shortstop was Curtis Wallace, who was as good as any shortstop I ever played with. He later made it to the majors with the Detroit Tigers, and last I heard he was a scout for the Seattle Mariners.

After that second out, I motioned for Curtis to move over three steps toward the hole. I thought I could get the hitter, a right-hander, to pull one that way. Curtis let me know he didn't want to move, but he did as I asked.

The next batter grounded one up the middle, just to the left of the mound and beyond the outstretched glove of a diving Curtis Wallace.

It was my mistake. If I'd left Curtis where he was, he'd have made that play. As it was, it cost us the game.

Bob Van Tine, the sports editor at the Kearney Daily Hub, was covering the game that night. He wrote in the paper the next day, July 1, that "Don Clark, a pint-sized cripple," was the pitcher who gave up the decisive hit.

Well, okay, I was five-foot-two (maybe five-three in the program). Pint-sized? If you say so.

And, yes, I wore a leg brace and used crutches. Cripple? I've been called worse.

But, hey, Bob: The name's Dave, not Don.

The guy did give me some credit, though. He wrote of me in the same article: "He amazed and thrilled the fans with his ability to pitch despite braces and (with) his skill at throwing strikes."

But can you imagine anybody in the news media today referring to someone as a "pint-sized cripple"? Thankfully, no, you can't imagine it. It just would never happen. And it should never have happened then, either. But, to tell you the truth, I found it amusing. I laughed it off.

Mom didn't think it was amusing, though. I clipped the article and mailed it to her, and when she read it she went ballistic. She called me and said she was going to sue the writer and the paper and maybe some other people besides. I guess I talked her out of it, or she just calmed down eventually, because she never sued anybody.

Apparently, my teammates saw that I was dealing with the article just fine. They even picked up on the reporter's comment and began calling me PSC for short. I thought *that* was amusing, too. For the rest of the season, I was PSC.

Pint-Sized Cripple.

CHAPTER 9:

AFTERMATH OF AGNES

Every year, no matter where I was, I called home on June 22. That's the date when Mom and Dad were married in 1951, and it's also Dad's birthday.

With Hunnewell in 1972, I was determined to call after a game we played that night. The game ran long, though, and by the time I got to a pay phone it was almost midnight. Too late to call, really, but it was still June 22 and I decided to try anyway.

I dialed the number and listened to it ring and ring and ring. No answer. That seemed strange. Somebody must surely be home, I thought. Why didn't they answer?

Now I was worried, so I made another call that I was uncomfortable making at that time of night. I called my grandparents—my Dad's mom, Dorothy, whom I called Grandma Z, and my stepgranddad, Joseph, who was Grandpa Joe. They lived in East Corning. My call woke them out of a sound sleep.

"What is it, Dave?" my grandmother said, and I could hear the concern in her voice. "Is something wrong?"

"That's what I want to know, Grandma Z," I said. "I just called home and nobody answered. Where could they be?"

Grandma Z explained there were some power outages in the area because they'd been getting an awful lot of rain. She said she'd been to

Dad's birthday party earlier in the day and everything seemed fine. She said she'd let me know if she heard anything, but I told her we'd be on the team bus for the next few hours. I said I'd try calling my parents again in the morning.

I had trouble sleeping that night. It bothered me that I hadn't talked to my parents on their anniversary, and to Dad on his birthday. But even more troubling was the nagging suspicion that something serious could be wrong. Why was no one at home to answer the phone?

The next day, when I came out of my hotel room in Monroe City, Missouri, I caught a glimpse of the local newspaper on a rack and was shocked to see, right there on the front page, a big wire-service photo of the Lodge on the Green in Painted Post—or what was left of it. All you could see, really, was the tall sign identifying the place, which was a motel and restaurant. Everything else was under water.

Now I was really worried. If that's all that could be seen of the Lodge on the Green, I knew our house was gone. We lived only two blocks from the Chemung River, which I knew was where that water came from.

It sounds crazy now, but my first thought was of our family dog, Bojo. I figured my folks and my brothers could fend for themselves, but I wondered what might happen to our dog. Then the realization struck: What if my family couldn't get out of there? What if the house was swept away in the flood? What if everyone *wasn't* all right?

I found a phone and tried calling home again, and tried calling my grandparents again. But I couldn't get through to either number.

Now I was close to panic. Here I was, nineteen years old, away from home somewhere in the Midwest, trying to concentrate on baseball games—*games,* for crying out loud—and I didn't know if my home back in Corning had been washed away and if any of my family had been taken with it.

Eventually, I called the Red Cross in Ithaca and got through. The woman who answered gave me a rough idea of the conditions along the river and said it might be a while before they were able to get any details.

"I'm in Missouri right now," I said. "I'm just wondering how I can get home."

"No need to try right now," the woman said. "You'll never make it."

Over the next week and a half, I tried repeatedly to learn more about conditions back home. There was no CNN or Weather Channel in those days, and no all-news radio stations, either. You got your news from the local paper, maybe hourly updates on radio, or the evening news on TV. Sometimes you had to go get it yourself. I'm sure I was a big bother to the Red Cross people in Ithaca, but they were the only ones I could reach. They didn't seem to mind, and I'm sure they were dealing with lots of frenzied relatives and friends just like me.

Finally, on the tenth day, I called the Red Cross again and was told that it was possible to make it through by car now if I wanted to try to drive home. I told Art Gaines about my situation and asked if he'd mind if I took a few days.

"Take as long as you need," he said. "Do what you have to do. There'll be a position here for you when you get back."

I was in my room, packing, when the phone rang. It was Mom, calling to let me know they were all alive and well. What a relief!

"I don't have much time," she said. "They've set up a public phone here in the middle of Denison Parkway, and everyone's using it to call out."

"In the parkway?"

"Yes. I had to wait on line for almost three hours to get my turn. Now I've only got a little while. We're limited to five minutes each. Then we'll be cut off."

So I kept quiet and listened. Mom went on to say the family had gotten out before the floodwaters hit. Yes, even Bojo had made it and was fine. The house had been knocked off its foundation but hadn't been swept away. It was destroyed, though.

The family had taken refuge in a travel trailer my parents kept on some property up on higher ground. The land belonged to a garbage disposal company that Dad partly owned. The family would be able to stay in the trailer until they could find or build something better.

"Were you able to salvage anything from the house?" I asked.

"Not much," Mom said. "Dan and your dad went back in a rowboat and were able to get in a second-floor window—that's how high the water was. They tied the boat up and picked through the upstairs, but when they got back to the window the boat was gone."

She said the rowboat had been carried away by the water, which was still rising. Dan and Dad had stayed at the window until finally an Army boat came by and stopped to pick them up. In the front of the boat there was a small pile of bodies the soldiers had collected on their rounds. Since Dad lived in the neighborhood, one of the soldiers asked him if he'd mind taking a look at the bodies to see if he could identify any of them. He couldn't.

Later, Dad told me that was the worst of the whole incident. He said he took a look at the bloated and battered bodies and nearly puked. Later, it was determined that eighteen people from the Corning area alone had died in that flood.

"What will you do now?" I asked Mom on the phone.

"We'll stay in the trailer for a while. Once they get everything dried out and cleaned up a little, we'll tr …"

And our five minutes was up.

Mom had told me there was no need for me to come home just yet. There was nothing I could do—nothing anybody could do, really. So I unpacked again, told Art Gaines I'd stay and play out the season, and I tried to put the flood out of my mind.

I never did stop thinking about it, though. For a lot of people who lived through the Flood of 1972, it has always occupied a corner of the mind. It was devastating—not just to Corning and Elmira and that part of New York State, but to a good portion of the country. Many people will never forget those sights, or those smells.

Hurricane Agnes spawned the flood, drenching our area—already soggy from a wet spring—with fifty straight hours of torrential rain. Conditions peaked that night of June 22 and 23, and the flooding began when a levee broke near Corning West High School, which is located near where the Tioga, Canisteo and Conhocton rivers meet to form the Chemung River. That let loose a wall of water that washed across the region.

Later, I learned that my brother Doug, who was fifteen at the time, had gone to the river with a couple of friends to watch the water rise late that night. Railroad tracks crossed the river at the site of the dikes, and Doug said a freight train had been left on the bridge, apparently in the hope that the loaded boxcars and coal cars would help keep the bridge from being knocked over—something that has never been reported, by the way. Instead, the water washed up over the tracks and backed up against the train, then pushed out to the sides against the dikes and finally burst through. When Doug and his friends saw that, they ran like hell. They stopped at a home nearby, found it locked and broke in as the wall of rushing water gained on them. Then they ran upstairs, climbed to the roof and waited for rescuers to find them. Fortunately, some of them did.

That September, after the baseball season, I drove home—or to what was left of it. I had an idea of what to expect, but it was nothing compared to what I found. The devastation became real for me at about Jamestown, in western New York. I was in awe of the destruction I saw, and the awful power of a flood that could cause it.

Every small city and town I passed on my drive eastward offered more of the same. Olean, Wellsville, Alfred, Hornell, Canisteo, Jasper—they were all in various stages of recovery. And at every place I stopped for gas or food or to use a restroom, the flood was all people talked about.

By the time I got to Corning, I was almost numb to it, but not quite. Corning was my town, no matter where I might be playing baseball at the time. It was where I grew up, the place I still considered home. What I saw as I drove into the city almost made me physically ill. Whole neighborhoods were gone. High-water lines could still be seen on some of the buildings that were left standing. The places where we once played ball as kids were no longer there. Corning was where the flooding had started in our area, and Corning had taken the brunt of the storm's fury.

But my parents and brothers and grandparents were alive, and to this young homesick kid, that was the main thing. They had made it through, and they would get past this. I was grateful for that.

Eventually, my parents built a new house on the land up where they had kept the trailer. They finished it in 1975—and one day before too long, it, too, was taken from them suddenly. No storm would be to blame this time, but progress, if that's what you want to call it. Despite promises from the man who was then mayor of Corning that a talked-about highway bypass would never claim the site my parents had chosen for their home, that's exactly what happened. When the bypass to state Route 17—now part of I-86—was built in the early '90s, Mom and Dad lost their home to the state.

Before this new home could be destroyed, though, Dad learned that you could buy your house back from the state if you'd agree to move it out of the path of the bypass. And that's what my parents did. They bought their house back and moved it thirty feet to the west. Then, finally, they moved back in.

And after all that, Mom died a week later.

As for me, well, the Flood of 1972 helped provide me with an off-season job that year. The previous two years, I had done door-to-door surveys. For two years, I pumped gas at the Teneco station that was then on Park Avenue. Anything to earn some money between seasons.

When I returned from Hunnewell in 1972, though, I got a government position inspecting the foundations of homes that had been damaged in the flood. I went around Corning, clipboard in hand, trying to look official but not having the slightest idea what I was doing. I had been given virtually no training.

More than anything, my new job allowed me to get a good look at what Agnes had left behind. It gave me a better idea of what I had missed when the flood hit, and made me thankful all over again that I had not had to live through that.

CHAPTER 10:

CLOWNING AROUND

My best season in baseball almost didn't happen.

In the summer of 1974, I was engaged to Shirley Ripley, the girl from Coopers Plains, just outside Corning, who tipped me off to the opening for a baseball coach at Corning Community College. We had met while I was a student at CCC and she was still in high school at Corning West, and by now we'd been dating for four years. It was serious. A wedding was scheduled for July.

My plan was to use my degree from Ithaca College to get a job teaching physical education and coaching. So I didn't play professional baseball that year, thinking my days as a pro were over. I was ready to move on with my life—or so I thought.

I'd had two seasons with Hunnewell, where my record was a combined 7–4 with one save, and another season at Fort Lauderdale, Florida, where I was 1–0 with two saves and a nice 1.73 earned-run average. But now I was a free agent. At the same time, I was looking at the end of my days as a free agent playboy.

I wasn't really comfortable with either situation. I felt there was still a lot of baseball left in me, and I just wasn't ready to settle down, get a real job and start a family. That summer I played and coached for the Corning Eagles in the Elmira Prep Baseball League, but that was just for fun.

As for marriage, heck, I was only twenty-one. That's too young—it was for me, anyway, and I suspect it is for most people who go ahead and get married at that age anyway.

Don't get me wrong. Shirley was a wonderful woman, and still is. She was the kind of girl you'd want your son to marry—very pretty, with long black hair and high cheekbones, and a terrific personality.

We had met one night when a bunch of us guys went to the office of my parents' garbage disposal company on Bridge Street and started calling girls we knew. A friend called Shirley and told her we'd pick her up, which we did. He told us Shirley was easy, the way guys do when they want to sound like they've been there. But I soon found out she wasn't that way at all.

Over the next four years, Shirley and I took in a lot of movies, spent a lot of hours at drive-ins, went camping and took other trips. She drove to New Jersey once to watch me play.

I had been raised a Methodist, but for Shirley I converted to Catholicism. As I said, it was serious.

Everybody seemed to love Shirley, not just me. She made friends easily—my mom and dad among them. She came to the house a lot, and my parents were always happy to see her. Even today, she'll stop by to visit Dad once in a while.

Shirley's married now, to some other lucky guy. She lives not too far from Corning with her husband and three children. She's a teacher, and I'll bet a good one.

No, there was nothing wrong with Shirley. If she had come along ten years later, we'd have probably gotten married and had a very good life together. But I woke up one morning that summer of 1974, just a month from the date we were supposed to be married, and decided I couldn't go through with it. We had everything ordered by then—the cake, the flowers, the gowns and tuxes, everything. The church had been booked, and the invitations had long ago been mailed.

Everything was ready but me.

I called Shirley the day I made my decision and told her I'd pick her up for a drive to Clute Park in Watkins Glen. The park sits at the southern tip of Seneca Lake, looking out over the big expanse of water, which was calm and clear that sunny afternoon. I love the water;

it's always had a calming effect on me. And I needed all its calming powers that day, because what I had to do wasn't going to be easy.

Several boats were anchored in the shallow water near the beach area, and some others—a few sailboats, a pontoon boat or two and around half a dozen motorboats of various sizes—cruised in the distance. Others came and went from the channel to our left, which led in to a marina and then meandered its way south to Montour Falls. Children splashed and played in the swimming area, along with a few out-of-shape parents and other adults. There was a volleyball game going on in one corner of the park, and the aroma of grilled meats wafted from a dozen charcoal fires.

I took Shirley by the hand and came right out with it.

"Shirley, I can't go through with our wedding," I said. "I'm not ready to settle down."

She was stunned. She had no idea what was coming. It hit her like a fastball to the head. For a moment she just stood there, looking a bit dazed, and then tears began rolling down her cheeks. I hated seeing that. I didn't want to hurt her, but marrying her would have, in the end, hurt her more. That's what I felt at the time, anyway.

So right there, we ended it—or, okay, I did.

I was no longer committed to a woman. My personal calendar was clear, my future was a clean slate again. And then it dawned on me: What do I do now? More specifically: How do I get back into pro ball?

That fall, I saw a classified ad in The Sporting News. This was back in the days when The Sporting News was still all baseball—earning its nickname, the Bible of Baseball, every week—and when it was published in tabloid newspaper form, not in the magazine format it changed to later.

The ad announced that the Indianapolis Clowns baseball team was looking for players. I knew a little something about the Clowns, but not much—basically, that they had been a barnstorming team for years. I was to learn later that the team was started in 1929 and played for years in the old Negro Leagues. In fact, much later I found out that the franchise was the last surviving member of the Negro Leagues when it finally ceased operations.

The Clowns introduced mascots and clowning to baseball. They provided a ballgame and a sideshow. And they played all the time and everywhere—in a cow pasture one day and a big-league ballpark the next. Their competition might be a group of "media all-stars" one night and a quality minor-league team the next.

The Clowns players hoped, like most players, to be spotted and signed by the scouts who sometimes attended their games. Every player's goal was the same: to join an organization that could move him up through the minor-league ranks and, hopefully, all the way to the majors one day. They didn't hang around long waiting for an opportunity, either. Most of them played only one season with the Clowns and then either moved up the ranks or moved on to other things.

I had the same dream they all had. So when I read the ad, I immediately sent off a letter of application, along with copies of newspaper articles to support my case that I could play for the Clowns. Not long after, I received a letter from George Long, owner of the team, inviting me to spring training.

Now I was back.

The Clowns were based in Muscatine, Iowa, in those days, and that's where they conducted spring training. I had just finished my first season as baseball coach at Corning Community College when I headed to Muscatine the third week of May in 1975. I drove out from Corning, accompanied all the way by the sounds of the Beach Boys and the great Motown groups on my car radio, and got there a couple of days early, as was my custom. I liked to look a town over, check out the ballpark, get the lay of the land.

Muscatine sits on the banks of the Mississippi River, and I found myself drawn to the water, spending a lot of my free time lounging at the river's edge. It helped me prepare myself mentally for the job that lay ahead. I spent a lot of time those first few days preparing my body, too, working out on my own before the rest of the players showed up.

I found out where George Long lived and decided one of those first few days to drive out and see his place, just for something to do. You never know what might give you an edge. Cruising slowly down

Liberty Street, I saw the number I was looking for but decided, no, that couldn't be Long's place, and kept going.

At the corner I checked the sheet of paper where I'd written his address, and that house was it, all right. So I turned around, drove back down Liberty even slower, and pulled over this time, stopping at the curb.

What can I say—the place was a dump. And it was in a block lined with other dumps. I was shocked. I sat there looking over the place, thinking there was no way the owner of the Indianapolis Clowns lived there. I must have written the address wrong. Finally, I decided to get out and take a closer look. Given the neighborhood, it seemed a risky move, but I was curious.

As I was climbing out of the car, I noticed an elderly man walking down the sidewalk in my direction. He was carrying a brown paper bag, munching on an apple, and juice dripped out of the corners of his mouth. I walked up to him and said, "Excuse me. I'm looking for George Long's house."

"I'm George Long," he said. "And that's my house."

And I was even more shocked than before.

When I told him who I was, Mr. Long invited me into his home. It was worse on the inside. There was junk everywhere—stacks of old newspapers and magazines, piles and piles of old letters. He must have kept every letter he'd ever received. Maneuvering through there on crutches without knocking the stuff over wasn't easy, but I made it to a chair and sat down.

Several cats roamed through the mess, and the place smelled of them and of stale chewing tobacco. Mr. Long's wife had a spittoon— yes, his *wife*—and she used it. We sat there in the living room chatting, the three of us, and every now and then she'd turn her head and let a stream of juice flow. She was a good shot, too.

George ate another apple or two, juice again rolling out the edges of his mouth and down his chin. The fruit looked soft and squishy, almost rotten. More like an over-ripe peach than an apple. When he offered me one, I thanked him but declined.

I couldn't help thinking that this was my new boss. This man owned a baseball team, *my* baseball team. What had I gotten myself into?

Well, if I thought the owner and his wife were a little strange, I hadn't seen anything yet. In a couple of days I would meet the Indianapolis Clowns, the players. This was the craziest collection of characters I've ever run across, in or out of baseball.

They could play, though. I was just hoping I'd show enough at the tryouts to have the privilege of becoming one of them.

Chapter 11:

Hey, Dude

The Clowns put their players up in a hotel in downtown Muscatine. The team paid for room and board as long as you hung on. If you got cut, though, you had to pay for whatever your bill came to from day one.

We were assigned four men to a room, with two double beds in each room. A very cozy arrangement. Too cozy. Invariably, the mattresses ended up on the floor, so that two guys wound up sleeping on box springs and the other two had the mattresses.

Camp lasted six days. After the third day, we came downstairs every morning to find a sheet of paper posted in the lobby of the hotel. The paper contained a list of all the players who were still on the team. We called it the Hot List. If your name wasn't on it, you were gone. Needless to say, we approached the Hot List with great anticipation, and also a sense of dread, those final days of camp.

Since not making the list also meant you had to pay your bill, players who were cut did whatever they could to skip out without being seen. One morning, one of the four players in our room found he'd been cut, and he was determined not to pay. He told us he'd give five dollars to anybody who'd help him escape undetected, and another of my roommates took him up on the offer.

Our room was on the fourth floor, looking down on the street corner. The player who'd been cut sent his accomplice down to the street and told him to get ready to catch two bags as he threw them, one at a time, out the window.

The player on the ground stood there, arms outstretched, looking four floors up as the first suitcase came sailing down. He circled under it, as if waiting for a high fly to make its way back to earth, and just watched as the bag bounced off the top of his head. He collapsed and lay motionless on the sidewalk for what seemed like a long time.

The player up at the window looked down on the scene and called out, "Are you ready for the other one?"

My other roommate and I took this all in from down the block, where we stood laughing our heads off. In fact, we were a little hopeful when we saw the suitcase knock our roommate to the ground. We figured, well, there's one less player competing with us for a job. Our spirits sank a little when he got to his feet, apparently unhurt.

He actually caught the second bag, and soon our pal upstairs had rushed down, grabbed his suitcases and disappeared.

Each morning I hurried down to check the Hot List, and each morning I found my name still there. Finally, camp was over and, one by one, Bill Heward called us into his office for a talk.

When it was my turn, Bill told me, "Dave, I don't bullshit anybody. I think you know that by now. You made the team on your own merits, but you're going into the season as the last pitcher on the staff."

That was good enough for me, and I told him so. But it wasn't good enough for Bill. He wanted to know that he could expect more from me.

"Can you work your way up?" he asked.

"Yeah," I said. "I can."

"Okay, then," he said, and that was that.

By now I had earned the nickname Dude. Everybody on the team had a nickname, it seemed. There was Popeye and Brandyman and N.C., who also answered to L.A. And Bill Heward was Captain Horatio.

N.C. stood for Nut Case, and he *was* one. He was from Los Angeles, which is why he was also L.A. There was talk that he'd been in a motorcycle accident at one time, and that when the doctors patched him up they put a metal plate in his head. Whether that was true or not,

I don't know. But his speech was impaired and it was sometimes difficult to understand him. He spoke v-e-r-y s-l-o-w-l-y and deliberately, and his words were slurred.

There was nothing wrong with his left arm, though. The guy could pitch.

But N.C. was, well, a nut case. He got involved with a girl one time and disappeared. I mean, vanished. We didn't see him for eight days. When he finally did show up, we were five or six hundred miles away. I'm not sure how he got there.

I was in the outfield one morning, doing some stretching exercises, when I heard this voice, deep and slow and kind of muffled.

"H-e-y, D-u-d-e," it called. "H-e-y, D-u-d-e."

I glanced around and didn't see anybody. Then I heard the voice again, and when I finally looked up and over the outfield wall, there he was. N.C. was sitting on the roof of somebody's house outside the ballpark, beyond the right field wall. Just sitting there, grinning at me.

"H-e-y, D-u-d-e."

We traveled in an oversized airport limousine, a huge vehicle with racks on top for luggage and equipment, and a large storage area in the rear. It hauled a trailer, but the spare tire for the limo was kept under the luggage compartment in the rear of the car, so every time we had a flat tire—which was fairly often, as I recall—we all had to pile out, unload the rear and dig out the spare.

We had a flat one time on a lonely stretch of two-lane back road in the middle of Nowhere, Wyoming. There was nothing as far as you could see except wide open spaces and, off to our right, a small herd of wild buffaloes. There were five or six of the big beasts, just lounging around in the sunshine, munching on some tall grass and not paying any attention to us. And that was good, because there was nothing between them and us except about a hundred and fifty yards of open field. No fence. Nothing.

N.C. looked out across the field for a while, studying the animals, and then said to me, "Uh, a-r-e t-h-o-s-e b-u-f-f-a-l-o-e-s?"

"Yes, those are buffaloes," I said. Then something made me turn and look into his face, and I saw an expression I didn't like. "And don't get any ideas, L.A. Those are wild animals. Leave them alone."

But he didn't. He couldn't. He watched a while longer with what seemed like great interest and then started peeling off his shiny red nylon Clowns jacket.

"W-a-t-c-h t-h-i-s, g-u-y-s," he said, and began trotting out into the field.

"HEY!" we all shouted at once.

A few players tried to get in front of N.C, but he slipped through somehow, and pretty soon he was out there in the field, maybe forty yards away from us. He assumed the fighting stance of the matador, or a fair representation, and held the bright red jacket out in front of him. He gave it a shake or two.

A couple of the bulls took notice right away. Then a couple more, as N.C. kept waving his jacket at them. One of the bulls put his head down, snorted and pawed at the ground. And that was all we could take.

We yelled to N.C. to get out of there and began hurling our gear into the limo. We loaded up in record time, and by then the buffaloes had started moving our way at a slow trot, then a faster one. From our point of view, it was a stampede. N.C. finally showed some sense, racing for the limo as we all climbed aboard.

The driver stomped on the gas pedal, and N.C. jumped in just as the car lurched forward, tires squealing. We all spun around in our seats and watched as the buffaloes came charging out into the road and, for a little while, chased after us. Then they quickly faded into the distance.

For a long time, we sat there watching, a bit awed by what had just happened. Nobody said a word. Then N.C. broke the silence.

Slowly, he said, "I didn't think buffaloes could move that fast."

Early in the season, most of our games were within driving distance, so we were able to return to the hotel afterwards. When we traveled longer distances, we usually stayed in hotels, but it wasn't unusual for us to spend a night, or at least part of one, sleeping in a park, sprawled out on benches or in the grass.

On the limo rides, George Long would usually take along a carton of milk, which he'd let sit there, out in the open, throughout the ride and the game that followed. Then he'd grab it when we got back in the car and take a swig. The milk was warm and probably had curdled by then, but he didn't seem to mind. He often carried some rotting apples in a brown paper bag, too—like the bag he carried when I first met him outside his house—and he'd pull one out and chomp into it as we rode along, juice running down his chin. He seemed to enjoy it.

Watching him, the rest of us wanted to puke.

I was paid sixty-five dollars a week that season, and we all got five dollars a day for meal money. We spent it at a lot of greasy spoons. Late one night after a game, we were seated around a large counter at a hamburger joint, ordering burgers and fries and cokes.

When N.C. got his food, he asked the waiter for some mustard. The man pulled a plastic packet of mustard out from under the counter and said, "That'll be ten cents."

"Ten cents?" N.C. said in that slow, slurred way. *"Ten cents!"*

I was seated a few stools away, and I watched this and thought: *Oh, brother, now what? Give him the mustard, mister. Just give him the freaking mustard.*

The man didn't give him the mustard. He told N.C., "That's what I said. Ten cents. You want it or not?"

N.C. didn't say a word. He just slid off the stool, left his food and stormed out of the place. The rest of us all looked at each other and knew that whatever was coming next wouldn't be good.

From my seat, I watched N.C. out front through the restaurant's large plate-glass window. He found a bicycle leaning against the building, studied it for a moment and then picked it up and hurled it through the window, sending shards of glass flying everywhere.

As one, the rest of us spun off our stools and ran for the door. We streamed into the street and scattered in all directions. The man who wanted ten cents for the packet of mustard came running after us and stood in front of his restaurant, yelling at us to get back there and pay for our food. Nobody did.

All that over ten cents. Crazy, huh? But to a Clown in those days, ten cents was big money.

Chapter 12:

Fireman of the Year

I made good on my promise to move up from the bottom of the pitching staff, and quickly.

Bill Heward used me in mop-up situations a couple of times, then tried me in middle relief in a close game once or twice. Nobody had claimed the closer's role by then, so one day Bill gave me a crack at it. It was the first time I'd ever been used as a closer, but it turned out I was good at it and I enjoyed it.

Now I was the top reliever on the staff, and it had only taken me a week and a half or so to get there.

To those who aren't that familiar with the game, a little explanation, because this was a significant step for me: The closer is the main man in the bullpen, the reliever who's called on to protect a narrow lead late in a game, often in a difficult situation, with the other team threatening to score. Not every pitcher can handle the role. It requires a certain attitude, a lot of confidence and a thick skin. If a closer blows a save or loses a game—or both—he's got to have the approach that, well, they got me this time but I'll be back tomorrow.

Without going into a lengthy explanation, let me just say that a closer is credited with a save when he holds down the opposition in a close game and his team keeps the lead and wins the game. Relievers earlier in the game can accomplish the same thing, but only the one who finishes up gets the save.

That season I blew one save. One.

I saved twenty games, won four and lost none, and my earned-run average was 3.57.

Again, let me explain for the uninitiated: An earned-run average is arrived at by dividing the number of earned runs allowed by nine (the number of innings in a complete game). It's the average number of runs a pitcher allows every nine innings. In other words, I gave up what amounted to just over three and a half runs per game, on average. Not bad, though not as significant for a closer as the total number of saves. When you pitch an inning or two at a time, or often just part of an inning, one bad outing can blow your ERA all to hell.

I was selected the Fireman of the Year in the Mississippi Valley League that season of 1975. That's an award that goes to the league's best reliever—the pitcher who does the best job putting out fires, get it?

As good as I was that season, I did have that one blown save. And, you know that part about a closer having to be thick-skinned and able to brush off the effects of a bad outing and all that other stuff? Well, you know by now that I had a bit of a temper and I hated to lose and I often reacted irrationally to defeat. So while I knew I might get the chance to come back tomorrow and even the score, I was not pleasant to be around after a game if I didn't pitch well.

I guess you could say that was the case after that blown save.

We were in Brandon, Manitoba, in Canada. The Clowns took a 3–2 lead into the bottom of the ninth, and I came on and gave up a solo home run that tied it. I didn't get tagged with the loss, because I was removed with the score still tied, but they beat us and I blamed myself.

Back at the hotel, I trashed my room. As I remember, I broke two lamps, the alarm clock, and two drinking glasses that were in the bathroom. There might have been more. In general, I left the place looking like somebody had ransacked it.

Then I went outside, still steaming. I took one of my crutches and whacked a lamp post with it. It was the right crutch; I was leaning on the left one at the time. The crutch wound up with a pronounced "C" shape, and I hobbled around on it for a while as best I could after that until I was able to replace it. Then it joined some others I kept around to remind me of a temper I needed to get under control. I would look at them and remember where and when I had wrapped them around what.

This particular incident cost me fifty bucks, not counting the crutch. That's what the hotel owner charged me for the damage to my room. Did I say ten cents was big money for a Clown in those days? Fifty dollars was ten days' worth of meal money. It really hurt.

The rest of that season, though, I could do no wrong. My knuckleball danced and dived and floated and generally left hitters taking weak swings or standing there just watching and wondering.

Maybe my favorite game that year was one I saved against the Muscatine Red Sox. Yes, the Red Sox were from the same Muscatine, Iowa, where the Indianapolis Clowns were based, and both teams played in the same league. And, crazy as it sounds, George Long owned both of them.

The arrangement made for a very intense rivalry. Those of us on the Clowns knew George favored his beloved Red Sox, and we would do anything to beat them, and beat them bad if possible. If we were ahead 10–1, we wanted to win 15–1. No margin of victory was big enough to satisfy us.

This particular game, we were losing 5–3 in the seventh inning when Bill Heward asked me if I thought I could finish it out if he brought me on in the eighth—in other words, go two innings. He asked because, as the closer, I usually pitched only one inning or less. But I'd gone longer, and I told Bill I could do it this time. As it turned out, though, he couldn't wait that long.

That same inning, the seventh, the Red Sox loaded the bases with just one out against our starter, the guy we called Brandyman. The reason he got that nickname was because he always kept a flask of brandy in his gym bag. He'd go into the dugout between innings, dig into the gym bag, take a drink and be ready to go again. Bill never caught on to him.

Well, Brandyman was in trouble, and so Bill called me in from the pen. We were in danger of falling far behind if I gave up a couple of hits at that point, but I shut the door on those guys. I struck out the first two batters I faced, and they left the bases full.

In the eighth, Bill sent up a pinch-hitter for me, and we scored seven runs that inning to pull ahead 10–5. That's how it wound up, and I got credit for the win—my fourth and final victory that season.

George just hated it.

I'll say this for George, though: He was always good to me when he talked to reporters covering our games or writing game preview stories.

For example, here's what he told Larry Taylor, a correspondent for the Augusta (Georgia) Herald:

"I've been associated with the Clowns for over thirty years and have seen a lot of pitchers come and go, and Dave would have to rank among the top five pitchers ever to don a Clown uniform. That's putting him in some pretty select company, considering that Hall of Fame member Satchel Paige and BoBo Smalls have pitched for the Clowns."

He also told Taylor, "Dave is a tremendous athlete and certainly worth the price of admission to see him play."

That season will always be special to me. Going from last man on the pitching staff to closer, and becoming Fireman of the Year—it was a dream season, really. I never had more than three saves in any other season, before or after.

I still have the ball from my tenth save, which I got in Holdredge, Nebraska, and my twentieth, at Ottumwa, Iowa. Those seemed like nice round numbers. I remember thinking as I packed each of them away: *You may never get here again.*

And I never did.

CHAPTER 13:

MISSING 'THE CALL'

After that 1975 season, I was at work in my office at Corning Community College one day when the phone rang. I answered it, and a hoarse voice at the other end asked to speak to Dave Clark.

"You've got him," I said.

"Dave, this is Bill Veeck," the caller said. "With the Chicago White Sox."

There was a long silence while I tried to figure out which one of my friends, players or staff members was pulling my leg. I knew Veeck, all right. Everybody in baseball knew him—and a lot of people outside the game, too.

Veeck has been called many things—a rebel, a hustler, a showman, a stuntman and much more, not all of them complimentary. But like him or not, everyone agrees he was creative, imaginative and innovative. Above all, he was a natural-born promoter, and a darn good one. No, a great one.

Veeck owned the Cleveland Indians for a while, and the old St. Louis Browns, and the White Sox twice. This was his first time around with the White Sox. Why would he be calling me? I wondered a moment and decided he wouldn't.

"Yeah, and I'm Babe Ruth," I said finally, breaking the silence.

This time *he* took a few seconds to reply.

"No, really, this is Bill Veeck," that hoarse voice said again.

"And I said this is Babe Ruth. What can I do for you, Bill?"

Eventually he convinced me that he *was* Bill Veeck, and I stammered around for a while, apologizing and trying to explain that I thought somebody was pulling a gag on me. He laughed it off, but by now I was feeling like an idiot. I let him do most of the talking after that.

Veeck explained that he'd seen me pitch that summer in Chicago and was impressed. The Indianapolis Clowns played a game at old Comiskey Park every season, and that year we won and I got the save. Little did I know the White Sox owner was in the stadium that night.

Veeck said he liked what he had seen and thought I might have what it takes to pitch in the majors. He told me he'd keep an eye on me, and he said if I did well again the next season he'd consider bringing me up to Chicago in September, when major league rosters were expanded from twenty-five players to forty. It was the time of year when teams typically gave big-league tryouts to players they felt were about ready to make the jump. Having Veeck call personally to let me know he was ready to give me that kind of break was a thrill in itself.

For any other big-league club owner, bringing up a Dave Clark would have been out of the question. But for Veeck, the idea probably didn't seem so far-fetched. This was a man who was always playing to the fans, and the fans loved him for it. He'd give out orchids to women in the crowd, tape gift certificates under the stadium seats, or send out circus clowns to coach at first and third. He introduced exploding scoreboards to baseball stadiums, and once he even let Browns fans make decisions on strategy by having them applaud for or against a particular move.

Far more important, he signed the first black man to play in the American League, bringing up outfielder Larry Doby to the Indians when Veeck was the owner in Cleveland. And he gave old Satchel Paige a chance to finally play in the majors when Satch—who got his start with the Indianapolis Clowns—was near the end of his great pitching career.

But people who don't know anything else about Veeck may remember that he was the man who gave major league baseball its one and only midget. That was in 1951, when Veeck was running the Browns, a team that was on its way to losing 102 games that season.

Looking for something to breathe a little life into the team, he signed Eddie Gaedel, a theatrical midget who stood three feet, six and a half inches tall.

Against the Detroit Tigers one day in August, Gaedel was sent in to pinch hit. He walked on four pitches, all of them high. It was the only at-bat he would ever get.

I knew all of that, and as I listened to Veeck I couldn't help wondering what he had in mind for me if, in fact, he brought me to Chicago as he said he might. Would I be just another publicity stunt, someone to amuse the fans if the team wasn't giving them enough entertainment? That's not what I was looking for, but I didn't want to come out and say so, not at a moment like this. And, thankfully, I didn't have to. Veeck assured me he wasn't interested in me simply as an attraction, a sideshow. He wanted me only if I could do the job on the mound.

"Can you get major league hitters out?"

"I sure can," I said.

In that case, he said, he would give me a chance if I showed the next season that I was ready for it. He wished me well and promised to get back to me.

So there it was—a call to the majors just waiting to happen. My big chance less than a year away, if only I could keep doing what I had been doing. There was no doubt in my mind that I could. It seemed so close, I could almost taste it.

Maybe I became too complacent. Maybe the success I had in 1975, the flattering call from Bill Veeck, and the fact that I had a comfortable off-season job at Corning Community College combined to lull me into a false sense of security. I don't know.

I just know that I thought I had it made. After that season, I didn't have the same level of commitment I've always had. For the first time in my career, I slacked off on my winter conditioning program. I still worked out, but not with the same intensity. I didn't recognize it at the time, but looking back on that period of my life now, I can see that that's what had happened.

I even got into a contract dispute with George Long. I asked for a fifteen-dollar raise from my sixty-five dollars a week after the season

I'd just had—the 4–0 record with 20 saves. George wouldn't listen to me. He said he couldn't afford me as it was, and he damn sure wasn't going to give me any more money.

"Well, in that case, I'll have my agent give you a call."

I can't imagine what I was thinking. I didn't have an agent, and I guess George knew it. Heck, I could no more afford an agent than George could afford me. But that's all you heard out of major-league players in those days: my agent this, and my agent that. It was still pretty new at the time, all the agent talk, and I guess I got a little caught up in it. Maybe I figured if it worked for those guys it just might work for me, too.

It didn't.

George growled at me over the phone: "Agent? You have an *agent?* (Bleep) your agent. And (bleep) you while you're at it. I got no time for agents. If you have an agent, you're off my team."

And he hung up.

Great. Now I was a holdout.

I couldn't suit up, work out with the team or have any other role directly related to the Clowns. So I stayed home during their spring training, hating every minute of it and wishing I could kick myself. When I couldn't take it any more, I flew out for the opener in Muscatine, hoping to clear things up with George. At first, he wouldn't talk to me.

While I was there, though, I found a way to stay at least marginally connected to the Clowns. I managed to hook on with the local radio station that broadcast the Clowns games, and for the opener I was in the press box, doing color commentary.

It was kind of fun, actually. I've always loved to talk baseball, so sitting there discussing the game as it unfolded hardly seemed like work. It reminded me of those days as a boy when I'd do play-by-play and commentary of my imaginary games and the games we kids played in our basement, on the street and in the fields back in Corning.

Yeah, I really enjoyed myself that day. Still, I'd have much rather been down there on the field. I ached to rejoin the Clowns.

I sat out one more game and then caved in and ended my brief holdout. George gave me the same sixty-five dollars a week I'd made the year before. I wasn't happy that I couldn't get more money, but it felt so good to pull on the uniform again that I almost didn't care. Almost.

Our next game was in Dubuque, Iowa. I was brought in to protect a one-run lead in the ninth, with one out and a runner at first, and got a rude welcome to the 1976 season.

The first batter I faced smashed a one-hopper right back at me, and I instinctively turned my head and never even got my glove up. The ball smacked me on the right side of the face, hitting me so hard that it caromed into left field. Right away, I thought my jaw was broken, but it wasn't, and after getting a quick look by the trainer and some pats on the butt, I was ready to continue. The next batter got a clean single to drive in two runs, and we lost the game.

I couldn't wait to hear what George had to say to me now.

Nice game, Mr. Holdout. Have your agent give me a call. I might want to cut your salary.

He usually came into the clubhouse after the games, but I was spared this time because he never showed up. We learned later that he'd just found out a handyman he had working for him back at the house had killed himself that night. Shot himself in the head in George's living room.

It never really got much better for me that year. The 1976 season turned out to be the worst of my career. I had only one save and no wins, and I lost one game. My ERA ballooned to 9.74, by far the highest I've ever had. And to make matters worse, my only loss came in our game at Chicago, with Bill Veeck again in attendance.

True to his word, Veeck called me in August. He said he wouldn't be signing me with the White Sox after all. He said he didn't think I was ready, and he was afraid that if I came up now I'd just embarrass myself, and he didn't want that—for either of us. And he was probably right.

I've always felt that, short-term, I might have had some success in the majors. I think I could have gotten hitters out with my knuckleball for a little while. But then they'd have adjusted, and I probably wouldn't have been around for long.

In the grand scheme of things, I guess I feel I rose to the level of competition where I was supposed to be. And that wasn't bad. All things considered, it wasn't bad at all.

Veeck's decision not to bring me up didn't surprise me. I knew that if he was a man of his word—that if he really wanted me only if I could help the White Sox and not just as a curiosity—then he wasn't going to bring me to Chicago. Not that season. So I thanked him for showing an interest in me and for being honest with me, and we wished each other good luck and hung up.

I've always been a self-motivator. Never needed anyone to tell me I had to work harder than the next guy. That's what had gotten me to that point in my career. That's what had put me on the brink of a shot at the majors. But for some reason, I had lost that edge during the winter of 1975–76. I've never understood why.

But I've always understood this: I blew my big chance that year. And I'd never get another.

CHAPTER 14:

WHEN IN RUSSIA ...

In 1977, after I was cut from Beeville, Texas — where I had the run-in with a left-fielder who tried to show me up—I received the rare opportunity to travel to Russia. This was in the days before the fall of Communism in the Soviet Union, when there was still a cloud of mystery hanging over everything having to do with that part of the world. Well, I guess there still is today.

Let me explain first how the trip came about. Like so many things that have happened in my life, it was a case of an apparent negative turning into a positive. Before I tried out for Beeville, I answered an ad in The Hockey News that said Concordia University in Montreal was putting together a trip to Russia to study the amateur hockey program there, and they were looking for people who were interested in being part of the study. It sounded like it could be fun, and challenging, and I've always been up for some fun and a good challenge, so I wrote in and asked to be included.

This was five years after the 1972 Summit Series between Canada and the Soviet Union, which opened a lot of people's eyes to the fact that hockey was alive and well—stronger than anyone had realized— behind the Iron Curtain. Canada, the birthplace and recognized world leader of hockey, had taken that series, but just barely. They won four games, lost three and tied one. And they had to score in the final seconds of the eighth game to keep the series from being a draw: three, three and two.

After I answered the ad, I didn't give the trip a whole lot of thought. I figured my chances of being asked to go were pretty slim. And the whole thing definitely was pushed to the back of my mind after I started the baseball season with Beeville.

But then the Bees cut me, and just a week later I received a call asking if I was still interested in studying hockey in Russia. There's the negative turning into a positive: If I hadn't been released, I wouldn't have been able to make the trip. Well, of course I was interested in going, so I flew home, packed a couple of bags and left for Moscow.

I made sure to pack my glove and some baseballs, and later I was glad that I did. In my hotel room, I spent my spare time practicing pitching—throwing across the room into my pillow. It was good that I threw a knuckleball and not a fastball.

There were seventy of us in the group, from all over the United States and Canada. We spent three weeks in Russia, mostly in Moscow. We did take occasional bus trips out of the capital city, and we probably saw things we weren't supposed to see—or at least we weren't supposed to know what we were seeing. Every now and then we passed what we all knew were missile sites, though our guides denied it when anyone asked.

As I said, Russia was a mysterious place, at least to those of us from the U.S. and Canada. I remember sitting in a restaurant one day with a Russian man about my age. I didn't know him; we had just struck up a conversation because he happened to speak English. All through the meal, the man kept looking over his shoulder, as if he thought he was being watched. It made me feel very uneasy.

The food there was awful, at least to this westerner. It looked disgusting and it tasted worse. One evening at dinner, I glanced down at my meal—a hunk of fatty meat, some strange vegetables and a bowl of soup—and saw a fish eye staring up at me from the soup. Every day they packed us a lunch consisting of a dry roll with butter, a boiled egg, a few slices of cucumber and more of the fatty meat. There was also a bottle of carbonated water to wash it down.

One afternoon I was eating lunch on a park bench with another member of our group when I noticed an elderly Russian woman standing nearby and watching us. For a while I ignored her, but when I realized she wasn't going anywhere I offered her my meal, which she was eyeing hungrily. She grabbed the container, gave me a quick nod of thanks, and gulped down the food. I guess if you're hungry enough it's not so bad.

We Americans spent most of our free time together. In fact, we were told never to split up. But one day I disobeyed that rule and wandered off by myself to watch a Soviet soccer game. It seems I'm always drawn to a game of some kind, no matter where I happen to be. I had to travel by subway to get to and from the soccer stadium, and on the way back to our hotel I got lost and didn't know which train to take. I'd written the name of the hotel on a sheet of paper, and I began showing it to people, asking if anyone could help me get there.

A friendly Russian man said yes, he knew the place, and he offered to show me the way. But this guy was a little too friendly. As we sat together on the subway car, he put his hand on my leg and I had to remove it. Then he put his hand on my knee, and I pulled it away again. Finally, the man asked if I would have a drink with him. And by now I was wondering if we really were headed for my hotel or if I'd wind up in a Moscow alley somewhere. Fortunately, the train finally pulled into the stop I was looking for, and I hustled out of there. Alone.

Back home after the trip, my career took a turn for the better. I signed with the Pennington Pioneers, an independent team in Pennington, New Jersey. They used me primarily as a starting pitcher, and it could be argued that my stats that year, 1977, were even better than in 1975 when I was the closer for the Clowns.

I won nine games for Pennington, lost four and saved three, and my earned-run average was 2.69, the best on the team. Out of twelve starts, I completed eight games. One night I struck out seven batters, a career high.

It was one of those seasons where you just feel like you're in the zone. Every game, I went to the mound confident that I'd have good stuff, sure that I could get hitters out. And usually I did.

My personal life was taking a turn, too. I just didn't know yet how much of a turn it would be.

I was engaged again, this time to a beautiful woman named Margaret Edger. She was the girl next door—literally. Margaret's house was next to the place my parents moved into after the Flood of '72. Following the Clowns season that year, I lived with Mom and Dad during the winter, and one night my brother Dan and I went to a hockey game and came home to find cars parked all over the place and our house full of people. With my parents gone for the weekend, Doug had decided to throw a party.

I walked in, and there was Margaret. We hadn't met before, but our eyes locked as soon as we saw each other across the room. She gave me a little smile, and I smiled back. I made my way through the crowd and struck up a conversation with her. Immediately, we both felt a connection.

Margaret had long brown hair and ideal proportions for her height, which was maybe a little tall. She shared my love of Beach Boys music, which was important because I liked to listen to music, especially the Beach Boys and Motown. Looking back, it seems the Beach Boys songs—the surfer themes and that wonderful harmony—formed the soundtrack for our relationship.

Margaret and I dated for about four and a half years and decided to get married. We were planning on a 1978 wedding, and so, as I had done when I was getting ready to marry Shirley, I decided to end my playing career. I wanted to go to graduate school and then get a job as a teacher and coach. With that in mind, I announced I would retire as a player after the 1977 season in Pennington.

The Pioneers threw me a "night" to mark my retirement and to celebrate my career in baseball. It was on August 20, 1977, and they called it Easter Seals Dave Clark Night. They held it at Roosevelt Stadium, a well-known ballpark in Jersey City, New Jersey.

My family traveled down for the game, along with fifty or a hundred other people from the Corning area. Dad was given the honor of throwing out the ceremonial first ball, with me catching. That was a pretty special moment for all of us.

We played the Giants from Livingston, New Jersey, that night, and I started. Maybe I got too caught up in the emotions early on, because I gave up four runs in the first inning. Then I settled down and pitched shutout ball the rest of the way, but it wasn't enough. We lost 4–3.

The next summer, Margaret broke up with me. I was home again, still in baseball but working now as the assistant general manager for the Elmira Pioneers. I still remember the date she gave me the news. It was June 19, 1979.

I didn't see it coming any more than Shirley had expected it when I told her I couldn't marry her. I was stunned and hurt. You don't know how much a broken heart can hurt until you experience it yourself. It hurts like hell.

The Pioneers played a game in Elmira that night. Usually, if I'm down in the dumps, a game will make me feel at least a little better, but not this time. I got through it, though, and started driving home. In Corning, I spotted Margaret going into a bar with some guy I didn't know. I parked the car, went into the bar and saw them sitting together at a table. I walked up to them, grabbed the guy without a word, dragged him to the back door and threw him outside. He rushed back in and came at me, but other people moved in quickly and separated us.

A year or so later, I walked into a bar in Painted Post to find Margaret sitting there with some other guy. I'd heard she was going out with him, but it still surprised me to see them together, and it still hurt to see her, period.

When I went up to their table, Margaret smiled at me and said, "Hi, Dave."

I ignored her, leaned over the table, balled my right hand into a fist and pushed it into the guy's face, just holding it there. I said, "You're gonna sit there and listen to me or ..." and he tried to get up. I wrestled him to the floor and we rolled around a while before people pulled us apart.

Margaret started screaming at me: "Get out of here, Dave! Get out! Get out of my life!"

That hit me like a punch to the gut. It took the air out of me. I just looked at Margaret, then turned and left without another word. If I had ever really thought we could get back together again, I knew now that it would not happen.

Still, I held onto the memory of her. For many years, I measured every woman I met against Margaret. It wasn't fair to any of them, or to myself, but I had no control over it. And so I went on looking for her in other women. But she wasn't there.

After Margaret left me, I decided to see if I could get a job playing baseball again. My position with the Elmira Pioneers was a part-time thing that I knew had no future for me. So I turned for help to an old friend, Bill Heward, who had been my manager with the Clowns. Bill had come to Corning in1978 to visit me and meet Margaret, to catch up on old times and to talk about a new project he was working on.

In the 1970s Bill had written a book on the Indianapolis Clowns titled "Some Are Called Clowns," and now he was working on another book, to be called "Exceptional Children." It was to be about kids who had overcome great odds to become successful, and Bill wanted to feature me. So he had come to Corning with a writer and a photographer, and I told them about my childhood and we talked about my days with the Clowns.

At the time, I mentioned that I planned to go back to school after Margaret and I were married. Bill said he'd gone back to school, too, but as a teacher. He was now an associate professor at Ohio State University, which is in Columbus, Ohio, and an assistant baseball coach at Otterbein University in Westerville, Ohio.

When I called Bill after the breakup, looking for some advice, he suggested I join him at Ohio State. He said I could be a teaching assistant while doing my graduate work, and I could also join the Otterbein staff as another assistant to head coach Dick Fishbaugh. I took him up on both offers.

Bill and I had some good times together. We worked when we needed to and played when we could. Dick was more of a straight-laced guy, with a wife waiting at home. One night we coaches went out drinking, and Dick got fallen-down drunk. Bill and I drove him home in the wee hours of the morning and were afraid of what would happen if we delivered him to his wife. So we gently set him down on the front lawn, left him there all curled up in the fetal position, and drove off.

I loved the college life, and the college girls. I had a different girl over just about every night. There was this one who was a steady, but the others came and went. My steady girl had a key to my place, but that arrangement proved to be a big mistake when she walked in one night and found me in bed with another girl.

Meanwhile, I received two phone calls that would re-ignite my playing career.

One was from the Delaware Valley Pioneers, my third Pioneers team. This was another independent team, and they wanted me as a pitcher for the 1980 season. We talked, and I signed.

Then, from out of the blue came a call from Sweden, offering me a similar opportunity, only better. The caller was a man named Bosse Hagberg, who was president of the Rattvik Bets, a team in the Swedish Elite League. He had read about me and wanted me to pitch for his team in 1980. It wasn't an offer for a tryout; it was an offer to pitch.

I didn't even know they played baseball in Sweden, and of course I had never heard of the Swedish Elite League. But I liked what I was hearing now: a four-year contract for a substantial amount of money—guaranteed—plus a free apartment, free food, the use of a car, and free travel to Sweden and home again.

I told Hagberg I'd take it if I could straighten out this one little detail: I had already signed with Delaware Valley. That contract would pay me only eight hundred dollars a month, and only during the season—considerably less than the offer from Rattvik. I didn't think I'd have much trouble getting out of it, but I was wrong. Delaware Valley held me to it, and so I had to reject the offer from Rattvik.

Hagberg said they were still interested in me and were willing to wait a year if that's what it would take. He said the offer was still on the table, now effective starting in 1981. He promised to get back to me the following year, and he did. We agreed then, and I signed for the next four seasons, not knowing that I'd never get to pitch even one-fourth of that.

I was disappointed with Delaware Valley, especially when they traded me early in that 1980 season. I went 1–0 there, then moved on to Clayton, another independent team in New Jersey, and I was 5–4 there with three saves.

Clayton was a terrible team, the worst in the Tri-States League. I remember, unfortunately, my first game there. On my first pitch, the batter grounded to short, and the shortstop threw it into the first row of box seats behind first base, sending the batter to second on the overthrow. Second pitch, another grounder to short, another overthrow, this time into the third row. I'd thrown two pitches, gotten two infield grounders, and had one run in and a runner at second to show for it.

From our bullpen, a booming voice called out to me: "Welcome to the Z League."

As bad as it was, I went into my last start of the season clinging to an earned-run average just under 4.00 and wanting desperately to stay there. But I gave up six runs in seven innings that night and wound up at 4.03.

I spent a lot of time that season thinking I could be in Sweden now, making what in 1980 was good money with excellent benefits. But I'm a man of principles. I knew the people at Delaware Valley were right: I had signed a contract to play there, and they had every right to expect me to live up to it.

And so I had.

CHAPTER 15:

WHEN IN SWEDEN ...

On the flight to Sweden, I was more than a little apprehensive. I mean, even more so than usual.

I've flown a lot in my time, but it's never a pleasant experience for me. I take planes because it's the fastest way to get from point A to point B, and often that's important—and sometimes it's the only way to go. But I hate flying.

On the long flight to Sweden, the fear of flying was accompanied by a concern about what lay ahead for me at the other end of the journey. Here I was, heading for a new country, with no friends there and no idea about what lay ahead—the language, the geography, the history, the social customs, and on and on. When I got there, I discovered that many Swedish people speak English, so that was a relief. But there was still a lot I had to adjust to.

Bosse Hagberg, the president of the Bets and the man who offered me the job with the team, met me at Arlanda Airport in Stockholm. He drove me from Stockholm to Rattvik through some of the most beautiful country I've ever seen, and we talked a lot on the three-and-a-half hour trip. Hagberg answered my many questions about his country and its people, and he put some of my concerns to rest.

But I still wasn't prepared for much of what I experienced that first season in Sweden, in 1981. There was culture shock, for sure, with topless beaches and nude beaches and, well, isn't that enough? And there was climate shock, too, with freezing temperatures and foot-deep snow—and that was on game days.

One fine day, a teammate, Christofer Ronnlund, took me and a cooler of beer out in a canoe, promising to lead me to a beach where beautiful women sunbathed in the altogether. I thought it might be a prank for the rookie from the States. But no, our journey up-river did indeed lead to a beach occupied solely by completely naked women who didn't seem at all surprised to see our boat floating around the bend. Christofer and I were so taken by what we saw that we flipped the canoe and spilled ourselves and our cooler into the water.

Women on the beach giggled as we splashed around and called to each other and worked to get control of the overturned canoe while the cooler floated away. I had always wondered if I could swim with braces on my legs. Well, I found out that day that, yes, if I had to I could.

I found out quickly, too, that there's not much that will postpone a baseball game in Sweden. The summer there is shorter than in the northeastern United States, where I'm from. Still, the baseball season there starts in April, and the playoffs run into September, and there's a three-week break in July while the national team plays in tournaments around Europe. That's about all that's going on in July, which is pretty much when summer arrives and departs. Most of Sweden—and, in fact, most of Europe—shuts down in July. If you need a plumber or an electrician or a mechanic, you're probably out of luck. They're all off on vacation.

Swedish Elite League teams play forty games in what amounts to about a five-month period, at the rate of two to four games a week. And it's rare that they don't keep to the schedule as it was drawn up.

On the evening of Rattvik's opener, I sat in the clubhouse waiting for word that the game had been postponed. There was a foot of snow on the ground, the temperature outside was around thirty degrees Fahrenheit, and the ground was frozen rock-hard. But that didn't stop us. They just got out the plows, as the Buffalo Bills would have done for an NFL game back home, and pushed the snow aside. Then we played.

I'm a warm-weather guy. Being from Corning, I've had to deal with a lot of cold and snowy weather, but I've never liked it. And I had never played baseball in it—not to these extremes. So I was not comfortable in those early-season games at Rattvik, or some of the late-season ones, and I've always wondered if that weather had something to do with the arm problems I would soon develop.

Each Swedish Elite League team is allowed to carry two foreign players, and I was one of the two on the Bets. But baseball is an international language, which is fortunate because I couldn't speak a word of Swedish. A fan from the U.S. can sit down at a game anywhere in the world—in Europe or Asia or Central America—and be able to follow what's happening on the field. But there are some cultural differences in the game everywhere it's played, and a player has to adjust to them.

One of the differences in Sweden is that players seldom argue with umpires. And in my time as a player there, players *never* argued with an umpire named Olle Svensson. An older man, distinguished-looking and very proper, with a long handlebar mustache, Svensson looked as if he might have stepped out of a photo of a 1880s baseball game back in the States.

As a raw rookie, in terms of my Swedish experiences, I wasn't aware of Svensson's hold over players. So one day, in a game when I was pitching, I got into an argument with him. I can't remember what got me going, but apparently I didn't agree with the way he was calling balls and strikes. I was in the dugout, watching as we batted, when I started hollering at him. Svensson called time almost immediately, came over towards our dugout and yelled at me to knock it off.

But I was really on the attack. As soon as he started towards us, I jumped out of the dugout, and we began jawing at each other as we closed the distance between us. Both of us spoke in English.

"This is a Swedish game," Svensson barked at me, "and don't you ever forget it."

"Bullshit!" I screamed. "This is an American game, and don't *you* ever forget it."

The argument ended there, and I returned to the dugout. Svensson called our manager out to inform him, in Swedish, that I'd been thrown out of the game.

The next day, one of the newspapers ran a cartoon depicting the Clark-Svensson confrontation.

The players on our team never let me forget the incident. I took a lot of good-natured ribbing about it the rest of my time with the Bets. Even now, if I run into one of the guys from that team, he'll say to me—in English, but with a Swedish accent—"Dave, remember, this is a Swedish game."

The players respected me, but not for arguing with an umpire. They saw me every day, running, lifting weights, doing extra work. They knew I'd had to work hard to get where I was, and that I was working harder than anybody there.

They saw the results on the mound, too. I had two wins, one loss and one save in 1981, and my ERA was 2.56, the second-lowest I've ever had.

I pitched just half a season, though. On June 19, the day before the All-Star break, my pitching career ended, unless you count a short-lived and ill-advised attempt at a comeback—and I don't. From that day on, all that was left for Dave Clark the pitcher was pain and humiliation.

I should have seen the injury coming, but I ignored the warning signs. In the days before I got hurt, I'd had a sore elbow but I dismissed it as something minor and temporary. Warming up in the bullpen that night in Leksand, my arm just didn't feel right. I can't explain what it was, but I knew something was wrong with me. I couldn't get loose. And it's funny but, as much as the cold had been bothering me, that was probably the hottest night of the season so far.

I got through the first inning all right, but in the bottom of the second I threw a knuckleball to the first hitter. As I released the ball I heard a pop and a tearing sound coming from my right elbow. The shortstop told me later that he'd heard the popping sound, too, out at his position.

I collapsed on the ground and waited there, in excruciating pain, for the ambulance to haul me away to the hospital.

Chapter 16:

Doctors' Orders

The first doctor who saw me said I had tendonitis.

Tendonitis? I'm no doctor, but I felt pretty sure that wasn't my problem.

As I understand it, tendonitis is an inflammation or irritation of the tendons in the arm. The tendons are chord-like connectors that attach the biceps muscle to the shoulder at one end and to the bone in the lower arm at the other. They help keep the arm in the shoulder socket, for example, when you do something unnatural like throwing a baseball as hard as you can, or with a sometimes twisting motion that's intended to induce a curve as the ball flies free. Maybe at the time of my injury I couldn't have explained it that way, but I had a general idea what tendonitis is, and I knew I didn't have an inflammation or irritation in my arm. Something had popped, something had torn, and I was in extreme pain.

After failing to cure my "tendonitis," that doctor sent me to a chiropractor—a decision that, in retrospect, seems every bit as foolish as treating me for an inflamed tendon. No, more so. *Much* more so.

The chiropractor put me on a table, grabbed my right arm and, before I knew what he was doing, gave me what they call an adjustment. It adjusted me, all right. I just about went through the roof. The pain was more intense that what I'd felt out on the field when the injury happened. If I'd had the strength right then, if I hadn't almost blacked out from the pain, I'd have jumped off the table and pounded the jerk senseless.

If anything, this quack did more damage. After my visit with him, I couldn't comb my hair or eat with my right arm for weeks. I had to use my left arm for anything that required any kind of movement, and my left has always been weaker because my left side was affected more by the polio than my right.

I still have a copy of a note the chiropractor sent back to the team along with his bill. He was an American, but the typed note was in Swedish. It read:

"Dave Clark has visited me for adjustment of his elbow injury with pain in the elbow and numbness down his right arm to the fingers. Dave has had these problems since June 19 and has prior to this been to a doctor in Rattvik."

That was it. Thanks for nothing.

I'd been hurt before, but never like this. Several of my injuries occurred on hockey rinks, including a concussion, a broken left index finger, a broken left foot, several deep cuts (some requiring stitches) and assorted other contusions and abrasions. In baseball, I'd broken my right foot, separated my right shoulder, had a rotator cuff injury and many times picked up scrapes and bruises while diving for grounders or throws in the dirt.

Once I cracked my sternum in a club hockey game in college. I was the goaltender, and as an opposing player came racing at me, full-out, a defender pulled him down from behind. The would-be goal-scorer flipped on his back and came sliding at me, skates first. One of his skate blades caught me on the breastbone and sent me tumbling.

I had to leave the game, but I was back the next night, against doctor's orders. The doc told me there was a jagged piece of broken sternum near a lung, and he warned that any sudden movement, or a jarring hit, could puncture the lung. But, hey, this was a tournament we were playing, and the team needed me.

I've always tried to return as soon as possible after an injury. Actually, that should read "sooner than possible." It's what professional athletes do, if they have any pride in themselves and their job—and most of them do.

You can't contribute when you're sitting out with an injury. And, besides, you begin to feel you're losing the respect of your teammates if you stay out for what seems like too long. You feel worthless, and you grow somewhat distant from the team. Whether it's legitimate or not, you begin to feel that teammates are looking at you—though no longer looking you in the eye—and asking themselves: "Is he really hurt *that* bad? Can't he see we need him?"

I played in that next hockey game after the sternum injury. We won the game and the tournament, and the injury eventually healed.

All the other injuries eventually healed, too. For a while, a long while, I thought this one never would.

A few weeks after my visit to the chiropractor, though, I began to get some movement back in my right arm. Now the team sent me to see a specialist, but he couldn't do anything for me.

Somebody then got the bright idea that if they taped my arm to restrict my movement, maybe I could actually pitch again. They made a brace out of the tape, running strips of it down my arm, from near my shoulder to well below my elbow, and wrapping more tape around that. It was effective in preventing me from extending my arm all the way, and thereby putting pressure on the elbow, and it actually allowed me to throw a baseball again.

That night, I threw on the side. It was a warm night, and I pitched the equivalent of five or six innings of a simulated game, working up a good sweat. When I was done, I went into the clubhouse and the trainer came over and began tugging at the tape, trying to peel it off. That's when we realized nobody had thought this thing through.

When they taped me, they didn't use Pro Wrap, which is what's usually applied under tape to prevent it from adhering directly to the skin. They had simply shaved my arm and taped me up. That meant I didn't even have hair to pull away with the tape—nothing but skin.

Now somebody decided that pouring gasoline on the tape might help to break down the adhesion, so they tried that. It worked on the tape, all right, but it burned the skin under it, leaving marks all up and down my arm.

That was the last straw. The Bets and I agreed that nothing more could be done. I was finished as a pitcher. After half a season of a four-year contract, I could do no more to help the team. But since my contract was guaranteed, they still owed me the majority of my salary over four years. And they made good on it, regularly sending me checks after I returned to the States.

In fact, the team was more than fair. They flew my parents, my brothers and my grandmother to Sweden to visit me late that season, and they put them up in a hotel and fed them while they were there. Then, after the season, the Bets had their annual team outing, a cruise on Lake Siljan (the city of Rattvik is located on its shore), and invited my family along as guests. During the cruise, the mayor of Rattvik presented me with a proclamation honoring me for my service to the team.

I couldn't have asked for better treatment, except for my arm.

Back home, I continued looking for someone who might be able to help with whatever was wrong with me.

Using my major league connections (I was still a scout for the Baltimore Orioles), I saw the team doctor for a major-league club (not the Orioles, but I won't name the team), and he told me about a new therapy that he wanted to try. It involved shooting water into the veins to bring relief to the injured area. He convinced me it might help, and I let him do it.

Water in the veins? What was he thinking? What was *I* thinking? That treatment did nothing for me.

Then I visited the doctor for another major-league team (again, not the Orioles). He urged me to resume my running and exercising. He said I needed to build up more muscle.

There was no way I could do it. When I ran, I propelled myself with my right arm, that being my stronger side. The way my arm was now, I could not put any pressure on it. Running and exercising—at least the way he wanted me to do them—were definitely out, and so was this doctor.

Finally, I saw the Orioles team doctor, Scott Teets. And finally, I got the correct diagnosis. What I had done, he told me, was tear ligaments, muscle and tendons in my elbow, some of them torn completely away from the bone, others just shredded. No wonder it hurt like hell!

"You were an accident waiting to happen," Teets told me. "I don't know how you propelled the ball. The fact that you pitched for ten years is just a miracle."

And to think, these other wackos were sending me to a chiropractor, wrapping me in tape, shooting water into my veins, and encouraging me to run. It's a wonder I lived long enough to get some real help.

Doctor Teets told me he hoped to repair the damage without surgery, and that sounded good to me. And he did it, too.

He had me go to Baltimore for one week each month. He even let me stay at his home. The rest of the month I'd go to the Sports Medicine Clinic at St. Joseph's Hospital in Elmira and continue with the therapy he prescribed, working with physical therapists Doug Frey and Dan Hartnett.

Teets worked me hard. He had me going ten hours a day, with an hour break for lunch. I'd start at eight in the morning and finish at seven in the evening.

No problem. I didn't mind the hard work or the long hours. I was used to working hard.

Teets had me on different machines, in the pool, on the weights. And I was running again. I kept up this routine every day all through the winter. And I could feel it coming back: I was gaining strength in the arm, and all over my body.

Come spring, I was outside soft-tossing a ball. Not what you'd call throwing yet, certainly nowhere near pitching. But I was tossing a ball, and I was feeling no pain.

I was actually beginning to dream of pitching again.

CHAPTER 17:

'A BIG MISTAKE'

All this time I'd been getting calls from a man named Richard Pohle.

Pohle was the manager of the Cape Cod Rockys. It was "Rockys," not "Rockies," as in Colorado Rockies, because Pohle also went by the name Rocky Perone, and the team was named after him. He probably owned the club, too, but I'm not clear on that.

I'd never heard of Pohle or Perone or the Rockys until he first called. It seems the team was an independent club with a loose affiliation with the San Francisco Giants, for whom Pohle was a part-time scout. He was assembling a roster of players who had been "slighted by the major leagues" to give them "a second chance," as the Corning newspaper explained in an article that announced my signing. The article said that meant players who'd had "successful careers in the minors or good semi-pro leagues."

Pohle (pronounced POLE-ee) was telling everyone, including me, that he was planning to take the team on a world tour. Mexico, South America, Asia and Australia were among the destinations he mentioned.

I'm not sure how Pohle knew about me, but in the baseball world word gets around. Supposedly, he had once played in Sweden himself. I say "supposedly," because I've never known how much of Pohle— or Perone—was the truth and how much was pure B.S. After all, his lies and deceptions have been well documented in many articles and columns in newspapers and magazines. Pohle has even written about them himself.

Various sources have reported that Pohle, who claimed to be from Lisbon Falls, Maine, was a journeyman ballplayer who in 1975 duped the San Diego Padres into giving him a tryout. He was thirty-six years old at the time, called himself Rocky Perone and claimed to be a twenty-one-year-old prospect from Australia. Wearing a wig, with makeup covering the wrinkles in his face, the bald Pohle/Perone actually got into one minor league game before he was discovered. The opposing manager recognized him, and he was released on the spot.

I didn't know any of this when Pohle started calling me almost as soon as I returned from Sweden. Here I was, with a useless right arm, not sure yet just what was wrong with me or how I was going to get it fixed, with no reason to think I might ever pitch again, and this guy wanted me to join his team. He told me he was having tryouts that spring in St. Petersburg, Florida, and he wanted me there. He kept calling me, kept encouraging me, and kept making the same offer.

The offer was this: I would not have to try out for the team. If I just showed up that spring, I was in.

That would have sounded tempting if I could have so much as combed my hair with my right arm. But I couldn't do that yet, and I certainly couldn't pitch, and I told him so. Still, he kept calling.

Meanwhile, I continued working out with Scott Teets, the Orioles team doctor, and also back home, following the program he had mapped out for me. I got a lot of help at home from Marjorie Lewis and her staff at Corning Hospital, and Frey and Hartnett at St. Joseph's Hospital in Elmira.

When the weather improved, I went outside and began playing catch with Dad, tossing a baseball over short distances.

As I progressed, I started using a softball. I'd always incorporated a softball into my workouts, because I like the fact that it has a different weight and forces you to use a different grip. When you go back to a baseball, you get the illusion that you're throwing harder. Also, with a softball I would throw on more of an arc, so the motion stretched out my rotator cuff.

All the while, the calls kept coming. Pohle wouldn't take no for an answer, even though I made it very clear to him every time we talked that I was hurt and there was no way I could pitch again—not now, maybe not ever.

He said he understood, but that didn't stop him. He called more frequently as the winter wore on, until the calls were coming every other day. When Pohle had no success talking directly to me, he began phoning my dad, which seemed peculiar for two reasons. One, my parents' phone number was unlisted. Two, I was twenty-nine years old by this time, so why would Pohle think he could get my dad to change my mind? Not that it would have happened at any age. Dad would never have tried to push me into anything, or prevent me from doing anything I had my heart set on. But this is how Pohle operated.

Why couldn't I see this was somebody I should never be associated with?

I asked Scott Teets if it made any sense for me to even think about pitching that spring.

"Dave, you've had a serious injury," he reminded me. "There's no guarantee you'll ever pitch again. Don't do this. Don't let anybody push you into it."

But Pohle kept pushing. And I kept pitching. Well, throwing. By now I was able to play catch from sixty feet, six inches—the distance between the pitcher's rubber and home plate.

The arm didn't hurt anymore, but something didn't feel right. I couldn't tell what it was, but it was something. A pitcher knows his arm, and I knew mine wasn't quite right. I knew I wasn't ready.

But was it something physical or just mental? Was it all in my head—a concern that something might not be right, rather than something *actually* not being right? Or was it, in fact, a problem in the arm? The questions kept nagging at me.

Meanwhile, Pohle pursued. And I began to weaken. He was the only one showing any interest in me, I told myself. He was the only one *likely* to show any interest again. I had the injury, I had the crutches—how many people were looking for pitchers with that kind of baggage?

One day, Pohle growled at me over the phone: "Clahk"—it always came out that way, in the thick New England accent he had—"Clahk, I'll tell you what. You come down to St. Pete as my pitching coach. You can keep working out down here, get yourself back in shape, and when you're ready you can pitch. How does that sound?"

I thought it over and decided it sounded pretty good. But just because he was so persistent, I asked for a twelve-hundred-dollar signing bonus. He countered with eight hundred, and we had a deal.

At the same time, I asked Pohle if he needed any off-the-field help. I had a friend named Ed France who was a pitcher on that Pennington Pioneers team I played for and who now was looking to get into the front office in some capacity. He might even still be able to pitch, I told Pohle.

"All right, Clahk," he growled. "Bring him down."

Late that March, I headed for St. Pete in my 1979 Mercury Zephyr. I picked up Ed in Morristown, New Jersey, and we rode together down I-95 to sunny Florida, swapping lies and recalling our playing days in Pennington. Having Ed along made the trip a lot more fun, and just thinking that before this was over I might be pitching again—well, that had me feeling pretty good about myself.

Pohle put up his players in a two-bedroom shack he was renting. Yeah, two bedrooms for an entire baseball team, plus him and his young son. And there was just one bathroom, with an old tub and no shower.

When Ed and I checked in, we found Pohle in one of the bedrooms with an infant that we soon learned was his son, Richie. He was changing the kid's diaper.

When he was finished, Pohle handed me the dirty diaper and told me to empty it. And that's when I should have grabbed my bag and said, see ya.

The kid's diaper wasn't bad enough; we had to dispose of Pohle's own turds, too. This guy never flushed when he used the toilet, that's how disgusting he was.

"That shocked both of us," Ed reminded me years later. "We both thought, what's up with that?"

And Pohle left such big loads behind that we took to calling him Logman.

Pohle ran a tight ship in what Ed now refers to as "Logman's hellhole." The place had no TV or radio, and it was lights out at 9 p.m.

That was more than Ed and I could take. After one night, we moved out and rented a condo, which was pretty rundown, too, with no air-conditioning. But at least we didn't have to put up with Logman and his kid while we were there.

The day we arrived, Pohle threw me a rubber suit and said he wanted me to get over to the field and start running.

"Clahk, I want you to run twenty poles," he said. That meant sprinting twenty times between the foul poles, from right to left, then back again.

I just looked at him. Run? I couldn't run.

"But I haven't run at all since my injury," I said. "I'm certainly in no condition to do that kind of running."

"Just what you need, then. This will get you in shape, Clahk."

I took the rubber suit and headed over to the Miller Huggins complex, where we were to train. Already I had a bad feeling about where this was headed.

All the while, I kept remembering the last thing Scott Teets said to me. I had told him that, against his advice and my better judgment, I was going to Florida to help coach a baseball team, and maybe—just maybe—to pitch again.

"Dave, you're making a mistake, a big mistake," he warned me.

"It's my last chance, Scott," I said. "I have to go."

"Then be very careful. Don't overdo it. Don't let him push you. You can't afford another injury. There's no question in my mind that if you try to pitch before you're ready, you will rip your arm apart again. And if that happens, it will be worse than before."

There was really nothing else I could say. We shook hands and I thanked Scott for all he'd done for me, which was a lot.

"Don't overdo it," I repeated to myself as I headed out of his office. "Don't let him push."

Chapter 18:

'You Got No Guts'

Over at Miller Huggins, I ran my twenty poles. I came in and had to just peel off the rubber suit. I was soaked and really had to struggle with it. I probably lost fifteen pounds of water weight that day.

When I returned to the field, in uniform this time, Pohle called me over and tossed me a basketball.

"What's this?" I said.

"What's it look like, Clahk? It's a basketball."

"I know what it is," I said. "But what's this all about? Isn't this still a baseball team?"

He had me take the basketball out to deep left field and start throwing it against the wooden outfield fence. I had to hold it at my shoulder, snap it forward with my wrist, and bounce it off the wall. Then I'd catch it or chase it down and do it again, over and over and over.

This was the dumbest drill I'd ever seen or heard of—up to that point, anyway. The other players were coming by me out there, ribbing me and asking, "What's goin' on here, Dave?" Damned if I knew.

"Just following orders, boys," I'd say, shaking my head at the foolishness. "Just following orders."

Finally, Pohle allowed me to actually throw a baseball. I threw on the side and then from a mound in the bullpen. As before, there was no pain, but something still didn't feel right. There was something wrong somewhere in my arm. *Something.*

Pohle kept urging me on, wanting me to throw more, to throw harder, faster, farther. Pushing me.

Ed France remembers Logman yelling at me: "Don't baby the arm. Dave, you're babying that arm!"

One day Pohle came to me and said he wanted me to throw batting practice. But he wanted me to do it at a distance of thirty feet, just half the distance from the mound to the plate. He sent me out to the mound and got somebody to place a hard rubber home plate on the grass out in front of me. Then he ordered the first batter to step in.

I could practically reach out and shake the batter's hand from that distance. He and I stood there looking at each other for a long moment, not quite sure what was going on here. Under normal circumstances, thirty feet would be awfully close range. But under normal circumstances for batting practice, I'd have had a screen in front of me to protect me from shots back to the mound. In this case, I had none. No protection at all. I stood there feeling a little naked.

"Where's the screen?" I asked Pohle. "I've gotta have a screen here."

"Ya don't need a screen, Clahk. Nobody's gonna hit ya. You can spot your pitches, work 'em inside and outside, and tell 'em what's coming. They'll hit 'em down the line one side or the other. Don't be afraid, Clahk."

Yeah, right. Easy for you to say.

The first batter was a powerful left-hander, one of the better hitters on the team. On the third or fourth pitch, he lined the ball back at me. It ripped the cap off my head and went whistling past me into center field. I never saw the ball after it hit his bat, it came back at me so fast.

"Damn!" I yelled, or several words to that effect.

Shaking from the close encounter and from the anger I felt, I bent down and picked up my cap and hurled it into the air.

"That's it!" I yelled, and I walked off the mound.

Pohle came out to meet me.

"That's okay, Clahk," he said, calm as ever. It wasn't *his* head that had almost been knocked off. "Come on over to the side. You can finish your throwing there."

Well, the workout with the basketball was pretty dumb. But pitching batting practice without a screen—and at a dangerously short distance—was the most idiotic drill I've ever come across. I couldn't figure out if Pohle was trying to kill me or if he just had no idea what he was doing. But I was so glad to get off the mound that I just went ahead and did as he said, and finished my work on the side.

Soon I was on a schedule of throwing in the bullpen every other day. My arm seemed to be getting stronger. There was still no pain there, but I continued to have that nagging feeling that the arm wasn't completely right.

Now we were getting somewhere as a team, too. The warm and fuzzy feeling from that first exposure to sun and sand and water had kind of worn off, and the workouts were starting to feel more like work. Just ahead was our first exhibition game, and as pitching coach I was looking forward to seeing my staff in action.

The game was at Fort Pierce, on the east coast of Florida. Ed and I woke up early, and I drove the Mercury, getting us there at about ten that morning, before the team bus. It was going to be a beautiful day, and it was already warming up nicely.

I went out to the bleachers, climbed about halfway up and stretched out on a bench. The sun beat down and warmed my arm and seemed to loosen things up in there. I was so comfortable despite the hard bench that I began to doze off. When I heard a gruff voice call out to me, I wasn't sure at first if I was dreaming or not.

"Clahk," it called. Then louder: "Clahk!"

"Hmm? What's up?" I said, coming out of my stupor and looking down to see Pohle climbing up the bleachers. "Something wrong?"

"Nothing's wrong, Clahk. I just wanted to let you know that you're starting today."

I didn't say anything. I couldn't think of anything to say that would have made sense. Did I have to tell him I wasn't ready to pitch? Did I have to remind him that I was with the team only as pitching coach until I *was* ready to pitch? Should I have said, in case he'd forgotten, that he had agreed to those conditions?

I just looked at him while those thoughts were going through my mind, and maybe he could read what I was thinking, because his demeanor changed all at once. There was a challenge in his expression now, and in his voice.

"What's the matter, Clahk? Haven't you got any balls?"

He knew what buttons to push, I'll give him that. Instead of telling him what I was really thinking, I changed, too. He had taken the offensive, and so I countered with what I considered my best defense. My attitude became, *Okay, I'll show him!*

"Don't worry about me," I said. "I'll pitch."

Pohle climbed down the bleachers and walked away, and I pushed myself up off the bench, rubbed my right arm and went down to the field to start loosening up.

It had been only nine months since I tore up my arm, and I remembered Scott Teets' warning before I left for training camp: *Don't let anybody push you ...*

But I let my pride overrule my head. I let Pohle goad me into pitching that day. I did exactly what Scott had told me not to do.

Warming up in the bullpen, I took it nice and easy at first. Then I began throwing harder as the muscles loosened up. There was still no pain; just that lingering doubt.

The game started, and I got two quick outs. Then I threw one pitch to the next batter and my arm went dead.

This was different than what I'd heard and felt in Sweden. No loud popping or tearing sound this time, no stabbing pain. There was no pain at all, in fact—*still* no pain—but my right arm hung limply and numb at my side as I stood there alone on the mound.

My mind was numb, too. Later, I wondered if I might have gone into shock. I was scared, very scared. I remember thinking: *Now what have I done?*

My glove and my right crutch had dropped to the ground, and I supported myself on one crutch, on the weaker left side, trying to keep from falling. Nobody came to help me. Then I looked around and saw Pohle walking out to the mound.

He came not to help but to berate me. There I was, my arm dangling uselessly at my side, my face no doubt reflecting the doubts and confusion and fear that were racing through my mind, and he walked up and stood in front of me with his hands on his hips and began shouting.

"You got no heart, Clahk," he said. "You got no guts. You've been trouble ever since you joined this team. I don't know why I brought you down here in the first place. Now get the hell out of here so we can get on with this game."

Then he turned and stomped off the mound and left me standing there awkwardly on one crutch, shaking with anger, so mad I couldn't speak. Finally I just walked off after him, hobbling on one crutch.

When I got to the dugout, Pohle was still going at it. He marched up and down, yelling for everyone to hear.

"He's off this team, and if anybody so much as speaks one word to Clahk, *he's* gone too," he said.

Nobody said a word. But when I got to the dugout, I went directly for Pohle and yelled back at him. I'd never talked back to a manager or coach before, certainly not in front of other players, and I've never done it since. But I let this guy have it with both barrels.

"You are a joke," I told him. "You are the worst coach I ever played for, and I use the term loosely. You're not a coach. You're not even a man."

He started towards me, and players got between us. I was defenseless, of course, with just one arm, and that one holding onto a crutch. But being the kind of guy he was, I have no doubt he would have hit me anyway if he'd gotten the chance.

And if he'd come at me, I'd have found a way to hit him somehow, with something.

Years later, Ed France remembered, "You wanted to knock that Logman out." And he was right.

Ed drove us back to St. Pete. I was in no condition to drive, either mentally or physically. He told me once that I barely spoke a word the whole way.

"I never saw you unable to talk or joke around," he said. "You were not yourself. I was uncertain how you were going to snap out of it. I knew you were strong, but I was a little worried."

Richard Pohle and I parted company at that point, and I haven't seen him since. That's too bad. I'd like to run into him some day.

CHAPTER 19:

HURTING AGAIN

I didn't see a doctor until I returned to St. Petersburg. Then I went to the hospital and got the bad news: I'd ripped everything loose in my elbow again and suffered nerve damage besides.

That's why I was feeling no pain—in layman's terms, the nerve was not carrying the message to my brain that I was hurt. The doctors told me I wouldn't feel pain until and unless the nerve regenerated, and that could take up to two years. They said it might not happen at all, though, and that scared the hell out of me.

Now I wasn't thinking about baseball anymore. My priorities had changed, and drastically. I knew I'd never pitch again, ever. Nobody would talk me into it again, and I was pretty certain that nobody would try.

I was simply thinking about life, and how I'd live it—with one arm, if it came to that. My arms are my legs, especially my right arm.

Because the polio affected my left side more than my right, I've always relied more heavily on my right side. Without my right arm, I couldn't walk, I couldn't drive and I couldn't write. I'd have to learn how to write and eat and do many other things with my left arm, the weaker one. Well, I didn't want to think about that just yet.

What made it so tough was that I didn't know if my condition was temporary or permanent. If the nerve didn't grow back, it was permanent. If it did grow back, all the way back, I was looking at a process that would take eighteen months to two years. That was based on the fact that the nerves grow back at the rate of one inch a month, and mine had to grow what doctors estimated was a foot and a half to two feet.

Somehow, I got back home to Corning. The details of that period of my life are a bit sketchy. I know I had the car, but I don't remember driving it home. It may be that I devised a way to steer and shift and brake all with one arm, but was that possible? The car was equipped with a special hand brake that I operated with my left hand as I steered with my right. I just don't know how I could have managed it all with one arm. And if I didn't drive, then how did my car get home? I really have no idea.

I do know that Ed France didn't drive me, because he'd already gone home, hopping a Greyhound bus back to New Jersey at some point. Somehow, though, I made it back to Corning.

Richard Pohle had offered to let Ed stay on and do public relations work for the team, but Ed declined. He reminded me many years later that I told him to take the job if he wanted it, and that I wouldn't hold it against him if he stayed.

"But I did not like the diapers, the logs, his bullshit and lies," he told me. "So I said goodbye as well. Logman told me I could stay and that I was making a mistake being your friend. He said you had a bad attitude and that I would be better off staying away from you. I still said goodbye."

In Corning, I found that I couldn't manage by myself in the home where I'd been living, so I moved back in with my parents. That couldn't have been easy on them—not only having me to care for but having me to put up with.

I was miserable at that point in my life, and miserable to be around. I became completely dependent on other people, and I've never been comfortable with that kind of arrangement, even in small doses. This was in big doses. For the first time in my adult life, I felt handicapped. It sent me into a deep depression.

One incident from that period sticks out in my mind, because I still carry around some guilt about it. Dad and I went to a hockey game in Binghamton one night, and I was using a wheelchair at the time because I couldn't put pressure on my right arm and therefore couldn't use the crutches. Having to use the wheelchair made me feel like a disabled person, somehow inadequate, and I hated it. It had me in a foul mood—even fouler than the mood that I was usually in during that period.

We stopped at a McDonald's drive-thru for burgers and drinks, and I can't recall what set me off but I started yelling at Dad about something and just got completely out of control. Dad has a temper, too, but he didn't come back at me. He just sat there and took all my verbal abuse. I guess he understood that I wasn't really angry at him. It's just that all my frustration started to boil over, and he happened to be the unlucky person trapped in a car with me at the time.

Thinking back now, I can still see Dad sitting there meekly beside me in the front seat, slowly chewing on his hamburger, tears welling up in his eyes. I guess I eventually burned myself out and calmed down, and we went on to the game and got through the evening. But I've always regretted the way I acted that night, and I think Dad understands that. I hope so. Through the years, he's remained my best friend.

At one point, I went to a nerve specialist in Elmira, a Doctor Mulki Bhat, who tested me and confirmed what the doctors in St. Pete had said. He asked me to come back in two or three months, and by the time that appointment came around my arm had begun to hurt terribly.

"Doc, this arm's killing me," I said when I saw him.

Doctor Bhat just smiled. "Good," he said. "That's great news."

"No, it's awful news. It hurts like hell."

"But it means the nerve is regenerating," he told me. "And with that comes the pain."

Doctor Bhat cautioned against getting too hopeful, though. The nerve could stop regenerating at any time, he said. It might not become whole again. I still might not ever regain use of my right arm. But he said the fact that there was some regenerating taking place meant it was now time to start rehabilitating the arm.

I went back to Scott Teets, the Baltimore Orioles team doctor. He chewed me out good for not listening to him and for getting hurt all over again, and I took it and knew he was right. Despite how upset he was, he agreed to work with me again, and that gave me new hope. I realized that if anybody could help me, he could.

Scott put me on heat and ice treatments. Three times a day, I'd use heat packs and ice packs, alternating the two. I rubbed salves on the arm and took the medications he prescribed.

Before too long, in that summer of 1982, I began tossing a tennis ball again, and later a baseball. I was working my way through the whole process I'd gone through the year before. And this time I was determined to stick with it, no matter what.

By now I was well enough to move back into my own place and live alone again. I love my parents, and I appreciated all they had done for me, but I needed my independence, and I knew they needed theirs. I was driving now and was in every way self-sufficient again.

The surprising thing, even for me, is that I actually began to think I might be able to play ball again. If not pitch, then maybe play another position. If not that, then possibly find some other way to stay in baseball.

Yes, I decided; that's what I had to do. As soon as I figured out how.

Dreaming BIG and getting my stance down.

Manager Dave Clark displaying the "hardware"
from another title in Leksand.

Dave, far left,
and the
"William Street Gang."

(left to right)
Doug, Dan and
Dave Clark.

The Cub Scout pack
and Dave standing
without crutches
at the far right.

The 1975
Indianapolis
Clowns,
Dave and then
Clown's owner,
George Long
(far right).

Getting ready to pitch
in Chicago's Comiskey
Park with the Clowns in
1976.

Putting a good swing on the
ball during batting practice at
Pirate scout, Art Gaine's camp
in Hunnewell, MO., 1971.

My 20th save ball
for the 1975 Clowns.
The all time
single season save record
for the Clown's franchise.

Dave delivering
a pitch for
the 1975
Indianapolis
Clowns.

Dave flanked by
Clown GM,
Ed France, (left)
and Roger Kahn
(right), noted
author of
<u>Boys of
Summer.</u>

Laying down
a key sacrifice
bunt for the
1985 Clowns.

Dave playing first base for the 1987 Clowns, stretching for the throw.

Dave and Clown co-owner, Mark Anglehart and the Jacksonville Majors, Stank White prior to a game in Jacksonville.

Pitching during my first season (1981) in Rattvik, Sweden.

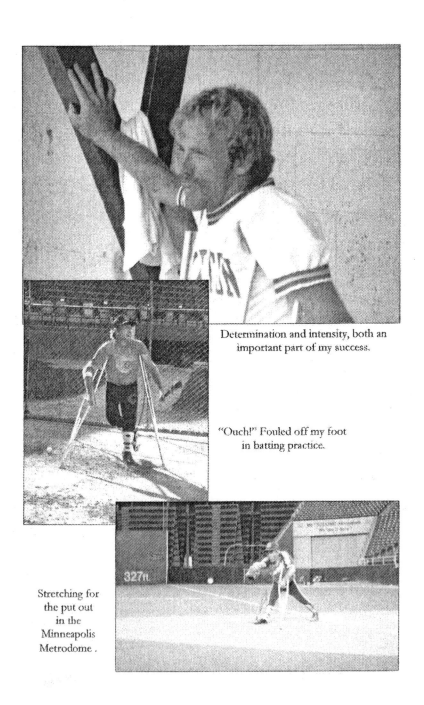

Determination and intensity, both an
important part of my success.

"Ouch!" Fouled off my foot
in batting practice.

Stretching for
the put out
in the
Minneapolis
Metrodome .

Hall of Fame member and former
Cincinnati Red, Johnny Bench, with Dave
and Ed France, Cincinnati, 1985.

Pitching for the Rattvik Bets
in Sweden, 1981.

On the mound for the Clayton Cougars in Reading, PA..
This was the last game Dave pitched in the U.S., 1980.

"No you don't"
another save for
goalie Dave.

Getting my own piece of
the Berlin Wall in 1990
with Camilla looking on.

Dave with
Anatoli Tarasov,
"the Godfather
of Russian Ice Hockey"
in Moscow 1977.

On the road again after another victory. The Swedish National Team, with Dave as pitching coach at the European Championships in Vienna, Austria, 1997.

A staff member of Team USA Baseball at the 1996 Olympics in Atlanta.

Dave, Sal and Ed with Pittsburgh Pirate great, Willie Stargell at Baseball's Winter Meetings.

Dave with for-mer teammate and star Swedish League pitcher, Magnus Hoglund (left) and long-time friend Andreas Ulanowsky (right).

The first year of Ocala Baseball Camp in 1983. Dave instructing pitching from a wheelchair. A pitching injury forced him off his crutches..

The Ocala Baseball Camp staff. (left to right) Camilla, Dave, Sal and Russell Dye

Dave and wife Camilla celebrating the Leksand Lumberjack's 1997 title in Sweden.

Elicia and daddy after a game in Sweden.

At the Atlanta Braves spring training in Kissimmee, FL., 1999, as a pitching coach at the Braves International Coaches Clinic, and as a scout.

Dave and his Swedish Elite League champs, the Leksand Lumberjacks, after their second of three straight titles, in 1997.

Coach Clark and the Swedish Junior National Team in 1998.

Swedish Elite League,
Northern Division All Star coach, Dave Clark, and his squad.

Coach Clark with his Swedish League Rattvik Bets.

Me with mom and Camilla.
The last photo of mom before she passed away in 1997.

Enjoying a hotdog in Ithaca, N.Y. at the same stand where dad got me one when I was a toddler, that made me throw up and get dad in trouble.

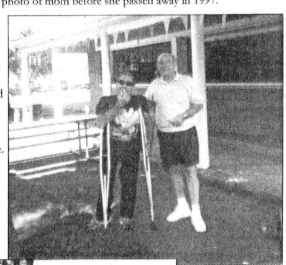

The Clark family home in Corning, N.Y., damaged by the 1972 flood. I learned of the flood in a newspaper story while on the road, playing in Monroe City, MO.

My Grandma Z
and Grandpa Joe
in their younger days.

The Clark family
in the mid 70's.

The Clark family enjoying dinner in Sweden, 1981.
(from left to right) Doug, Grandma Z, Dad, Mom, me and Dan.

Dad, family friend Emma Cornelius, tiny Elicia on the table, Camilla and me out for Friday Night Fish Fry.

Dave's maternal grandparents, Bertha and Jim Strawser.

Mom (right) and her sister, my aunt Marg. We grew up playing together and were in the same high school graduating class.

Mom, Camilla, me and dad enjoying a gondola ride in Venice, Italy after the 1990 season in Sweden.

Dave, an Elmira Pioneers coach, and expectant wife, Camilla, at Dunn Field, Elmira, N. Y., 1999.

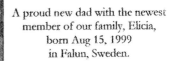

A proud new dad with the newest member of our family, Elicia, born Aug 15, 1999 in Falun, Sweden.

Elicia's first Christmas with mommy and daddy.

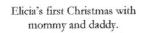

Me, Elicia and Camilla with Per, Nathalie and Eva, my Swedish in-laws.

Camilla with her Aunt, dad, sister Bea, brother Tobbe and sister Kim.

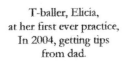

T-baller, Elicia, at her first ever practice, In 2004, getting tips from dad.

Dad and daughter, Elicia, enjoying a scooter ride on Dave's first scooter in 2000.

Daughter Elicia with Dave's first pair of leg braces that he wore when he was two years old.

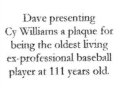

Dave presenting Cy Williams a plaque for being the oldest living ex-professional baseball player at 111 years old.

Dave being congratulated by President Bill Clinton at the White House on winning The Giant Steps Coaching Award in April of 1996.

THE WHITE HOUSE

WASHINGTON

May 10, 1996

<u>PERSONAL</u>

Mr. Dave Clark
Apartment 2E
101 Davis Street
Corning, New York 14830

Dear Dave:

    Thanks for the poster. I appreciate your generosity and thoughtfulness, and I am glad you were able to join us at the White House as we recognized National Student Athlete Day. Hillary joins me in sending best wishes to you and everyone at the Indianapolis Clowns Baseball Club.

Sincerely,

Bill Clinton

(left to right) Dad holding my SGMA Heroes Award, me, Camilla
and the late Dick Shapp holding Elicia.

Dave receiving
the 'Key to the City"
of his hometown,
Corning, N.Y. from
Mayor Al Lewis
in 1996.

Dave's Ithaca
College Athletic
Hall of Fame
induction, 2002.

Our first Baseball Camp for the Mentally Challenged,
and these camps are still going!

Life long friends
Mick Moshier,
Dave Gronski, me and
my cousin Tim Strawser
hanging around before
the Crystal City
Classic Cup Tourney
in Corning, N.Y., 1978.

Dave and
broadcast partner
Tom Callahan calling
the Elmira Jackals
professional hockey.

Dave and Sal with the late Herb Brooks, coach of the 1980 USA Olympic Gold Medal "Miracle on Ice" hockey team.

Dave and dad at game 7 of the 2004 Stanley Cup Finals watching the Tampa Bay Lightning "take it all".

Dave donating some of his artifacts to the Cooperstown Baseball Hall of Fame Librarian, Jim Gates in 1997.

That speck in the sky is me, para-sailing in Cancun, Mexico, 1994.

Speaking at the
Baseball Hall of Fame
in Cooperstown, N.Y.

Dave, Corning
(N.Y.) Community
College's first
baseball coach,
with assistant
Jim Allen.

L.A. Dodger great,
Don Drysdale
with Sal and I in 1984.

Going horizontal to snare a line
drive while playing first base for
the Clowns in 1986.

The 1988 Indianapolis Clowns, the final year.

Trying my hand at downhill skiing in 1992.

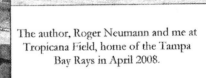

The author, Roger Neumann and me at Tropicana Field, home of the Tampa Bay Rays in April 2008.

The Indianapolis Clowns Reunion at Dunn Field, Elmira, N.Y., 2005. (Front row) Sal and Dave, (back row) Ron Lindensmith, Dave Stalbird, Ed France, Al Tobin, Dave Geis and Tim Strawser.

Chapter 20:

Mr. Businessman

The idea for my next move actually started taking shape while I was still living with my parents.

I remember lounging around the pool in their back yard, my right arm in a sling, and thinking back to the days when I was a reliever and those of us out in the bullpen would pass the time talking about anything and everything. Girls, mostly, but other things too.

Steve Altman was a guy I always liked to have around for those bull sessions. Steve was another reliever, and we pitched together with Clayton and with the Clowns. One night when we were with Clayton, there was a blackout during the game, and I mean black. When the lights went out, you couldn't see anything. I took one of my crutches, pointed it at Steve and made a sound that I thought imitated a rifle shot. Steve grabbed the other crutch and pretended to fire back.

Pretty soon we were crawling around on the ground like a couple of kids, firing our crutches at each other and anything else that we suspected of being the enemy, or at least a good target. We scrambled out of the bullpen and crawled on our elbows and knees across the outfield grass, while the darkness stretched on for several minutes and the only sound was a murmur from the fans in the grandstand across the field.

Then, without warning, the lights came on. Everyone was surprised to see two players in the outfield, stretched out on the grass, each with a crutch under his shoulder, taking aim at, well, something. Steve and I hustled back to the bullpen, and the game resumed.

When Steve and I weren't similarly horsing around, we were thinking and talking about our futures. We had both decided that we wanted to stay in baseball after our playing days were over. But how? That was always the question.

One of us came up with the idea of running a baseball camp. That appealed to both of us because, for one thing, it would put us in positions of responsibility and authority and, for another, it would allow us to work with and help develop young players. The more we talked about the idea, the more appealing it sounded.

That day at the pool in my parents' yard, I thought about the conversations Steve and I used to have. And I was not surprised to find that the idea of a baseball camp still was appealing. I kept working it over in my mind as my condition improved, and the better I felt the more I found myself thinking about baseball.

One day I called Steve at his home in Chicago. He was coaching a high school baseball team, but as soon as we started reviving the old baseball camp talk, I could tell he was still interested, too. We talked about actually doing it—buying a camp or starting one—and the more we talked the more excited we both became.

"There's a place in Ocala, Florida, that we ought to look into," I told Steve. "It used to be a camp, but I think it's closed now."

I had driven past the complex when I was in Florida, and I'd stopped to talk to someone about it. The place was the former spring training home of the Boston Red Sox, and it had been closed for a year or so. Unless someone else had reopened it since I'd looked it over, I thought it would be perfect for us.

"Maybe we ought to go down there and check it out," Steve said, and I knew he was ready to move on this. So was I.

We went to Ocala, learned that the city owned the complex, talked to the official with responsibility for the property, and found out that it was available. The place had all we needed—four fields, a clubhouse and even a grounds crew that was provided by the city. The rent was five hundred dollars a week, which we considered reasonable.

We took it.

The Ocala Baseball Camp opened in February of 1983 with a bankroll of five thousand dollars. Five investors put up a thousand each, including Steve and me. The others were my Dad, my brother Dan and a good friend from Corning named Sal Tombasco, who had played for me at Corning Community College.

Lots of other people had the opportunity to get in on the deal, but they decided against it. Some of them later told me they regretted that decision, and I don't doubt they did. The camp became very successful.

I've always been a baseball man, not a businessman. But, as I've said before, I've got an analytical mind, and I just applied it to business issues as I had always applied it to other things. Naturally, it helped that our business was still baseball. But, really, I think business sense is basically common sense, and that's how I approached our new business.

That first year, I lined up a working agreement with the Utica Blue Sox, an independent team in upstate New York that played in the Class A New York-Penn League. The Blue Sox are probably best known for being partly owned by author Roger Kahn, who wrote "The Boys of Summer," a very entertaining book about the old Brooklyn Dodgers, and other books. Our job at the camp was to give young players an opportunity to try out for the Blue Sox.

I advertised in baseball publications for individual players to come to our camp, and for college and high school teams to use Ocala as a base of operations for a spring trip to Florida. The appeal for the teams was that they could practice and play games at the main field, Gerig Stadium—not Gehrig, as in Lou, but Gerig, as in the local politician for whom it was named—and we would set up a schedule of games for them. All they had to do was get there. It turned out to be a great arrangement for them and good for us, but a hell of a lot of work for me.

Before we could get started, we had to put a lot of money into the camp. It needed a bunch of new equipment, including batting cages. The fields had the metal frames for the cages but no netting. So we stocked up on what we needed.

The complex was located in a seedy part of town, and we were warned that every night we should take with us anything that wasn't tied down, and tie down anything we couldn't take with us. We got a little careless, I guess, and the third day at camp we discovered someone had cut the netting in half in all the batting cages. Also, the clubhouse door had been forced open, and equipment had been taken from inside. In all, the value of what we lost came to around three thousand dollars.

Welcome to Ocala.

We took the netting in the batting cages and tied the two halves together, and that worked sufficiently. But from that day on, we removed all the equipment, including the nets, and piled it into the camp bus every night and drove it away with us.

Despite the thievery, we turned a profit that first year. And we continued to operate the camp successfully for eleven years in all, and to make good money from it. Finally, though, the camp had run its course for us, and we shut it down in 1994.

CHAPTER 21:

WE OWN THE CLOWNS

When camp ended in April that first year, 1983, we all went back home.

My arm was still hurting, so I went to the Sports Medicine Clinic at St. Joseph's Hospital in Elmira and worked out under the care of Doug Frey and Dan Harknett. I kept a log of my progress, which helps me now to remember just how far I was from being able to play ball again.

On May 10, according to my log, I tried lifting five-pound free weights but couldn't manage it.

"It put strain on elbow ulnar area," I wrote. And I added, "Wrist pain."

Instead of five pounds, I lifted two-pound weights in four different motions.

"Arm sore, tired and somewhat tight," I wrote in the log. "Used ice and heat afterward."

I wrote that Dan put pads on my crutches and suggested I lower the crutches to ease the pressure on my arms when I walked.

Three days later, I was lifting three-pound weights—apparently a sign of some progress. But I continued to note my discomfort: tightness, numbness, a pinched feeling, and plenty of just plain aches and pains.

"Arm feeling a bit stronger today," I wrote on May 17. But I added that I still had pain around the elbow.

The following day, I graduated to four-pound weights, "with no apparent side effects." I wrote that the doctor and I were both pleased.

Then, in what appears to be something I added later that day: "However, my left arm has been numb all day and at times has felt partially paralyzed. This has definitely got me concerned. WHAT NEXT!!"

I rested the arm for several days, and then tried to run on June 2. Here's what I wrote later:

"Afterward experienced some (felt like nerve) discomfort around wrist bone and elbow. Also, hand seems to get cold and change colors when I aggravate something."

On June 6, I went through the weight-lifting routine again, but this time without the weights. Just going through the motions. There was still some pain, though nothing serious.

At nine that night, I added this note:

"Turned elbow and arm over with palm toward sky. Bounced elbow a bit and something snapped, instant pain. Iced immediately.

"Am down mentally."

I kept the log going until mid-June. This was my final entry, for June 13–14:

"Coldness in elbow area (often). Started swimming exercises with no adverse effect so far."

Through it all, I kept thinking about how I could get back into baseball. I mean, something beyond the camp. I know that sounds crazy, but I did it nevertheless.

One fine summer afternoon, Sal and I were out in a boat, fishing on Seneca Lake near Watkins Glen, our minds as much on baseball as on the bass we were targeting. The talk got around to what we could do to fill up the rest of the year after camp closed.

"What if we had our own team?" I said.

"What do you mean?" Sal said. "What kind of team?"

"I don't know. An independent team. Maybe a traveling team, like the Clowns."

"A barnstorming team?"

"Yeah. We could use the camp to try out players, then go right from camp to a season on the road."

Sal liked the idea, and so did I.

We worked it over in our minds a little, talked it through a bit more, and agreed it might be worth a try. The only part we didn't care for was the idea of starting a new team, and all the uncertainty that went with it. What would we call the team? Would people come out to see a game played by a team they'd never heard of? How would we get our name out there in front of the public?

We had lots of questions but few answers.

About a month went by, the idea still churning in our minds, when I received a letter from George Long, the owner of the Clowns. He wrote to say that he had decided to sell the team and, in fact, already had an interested buyer. I hadn't mentioned to him that Sal and I were interested in starting a team like the Clowns, so I have no idea why he thought to write to me. He just said in the letter that he thought I might want to know.

I called George right away.

"What will it take to get the Clowns?" I asked.

"I've been offered twenty-five thousand," he said. "I'd like you to have the team, though, Dave. If you can match that, it's yours."

I told George I was interested and said I'd get back to him. Then I talked over the idea with Sal, and we decided to go for it. We didn't have the money, not all of it, but we were pretty sure we could come up with it. A few days later I called George and told him we wanted the team.

Sal and I lined up another partner, Mark Anglehart, who also lived in Corning, and my Dad bought in for a small piece. When we closed the deal that September, we all became owners of the Indianapolis Clowns.

This was not like starting our own team, and I don't mean just from the standpoint of having name recognition. The Clowns had a history and a reputation, and we respected those things and vowed to uphold them.

The recorded history of the Clowns is very sketchy, but we know the roots of the team stretch back to the old Negro Leagues. Those were the leagues, starting with the Negro National League in 1920, that were formed for black players because white team owners and league officials wouldn't let them play in the major leagues—or, for that matter, in the minors. The Clowns were founded in 1929, apparently by blacks, as a barnstorming team that would travel across the United States and Canada, playing local teams at mostly small-town stops along the way.

First, the team was called either the Miami Clowns or the Canadian Clowns, or maybe both. It might be they used one name for their U.S. stops and the other when they played in Canada. Again, what we know of those early years is limited and sometimes conflicting. We do know they earned their billing as "baseball's most popular comic attraction" and they also played some solid baseball—starting long before we bought the team and continuing while we were the owners.

The team joined the Negro American League in 1941 or '43. Some of black baseball's biggest stars wore the Clowns uniform, including Satchel Paige and Buck O'Neil. Toni Stone was believed to be the first woman in a men's professional baseball league when she played for the Clowns in 1952.

Hank Aaron signed with the Clowns for two hundred and fifty dollars a month in 1952, plus a suitcase as a bonus. But by then Jackie Robinson had broken baseball's color barrier, and just six weeks after Aaron joined the Clowns his contract was sold to the old Boston Braves of the National League. Aaron played for the Braves when the team was in Milwaukee and then Atlanta, and he went into the Baseball Hall of Fame as the game's all-time career home run leader.

Sal, Mark, Dad and I became just the fourth owners of the Clowns. Now, when the Ocala Baseball Camp opened for its second year a few months after we bought the team, we offered players an opportunity to try out for both the Clowns and the Utica Blue Sox.

They came at the rate of about thirty players a week. The camp lasted about three months, and by the end of that time we had a full roster and some backups for the Clowns, and we were able to send some players to Utica. Plus, we continued to draw high school and college teams to the camp.

It was the perfect situation for us.

It was a very good situation for Dave Clark the ballplayer, too. I continued to work out, continued to strengthen my arm, and continued to dream of playing baseball again. I saw the Clowns as an opportunity to do so at my own pace and at a position of my choosing.

I chose first base because it suited me best at this stage of my career. Rarely would I have to throw any distance at all; I was a small target but good with the glove; and in most cases, I wouldn't have to cover much ground. So I started working out at first base and, eventually, playing there for the Clowns in spring games. We played exhibition games against the college teams in camp, semi-pro teams in the area, and minor league teams from the Florida State League.

Tim Walsh, one of the Clowns players who went through the camp, wrote many years later of his first thoughts after meeting me:

"Dave's confidence and self-assurance were immediately apparent the first time I met him. But my first thoughts were, who is this guy and what in the hell am I doing here? Then I heard Dave was not only going to manage the Clowns but that he was going to play, too. Well, calling him an athlete, a baseball player, that was just too much of a stretch for me at that time. How wrong I was.

"Dave was short by first basemen's standards, but he was the best at digging low throws out of the dirt. What hands he had. He performed magic over and over, night after night, with the plays he made at first base.

"My only regret is that I never got to see Dave pitch. He injured his pitching arm long before we became associated with each other. Years later, I did see a tape of Dave pitching. It remains one of the most jaw-dropping pieces of athletic footage I have ever seen."

With the Clowns, I also handled the signing of players, the scheduling of games, the promotion of the team and a thousand other details. In a way, it was like being a kid back in Corning again, running our neighborhood teams and my imaginary leagues. Except back then I not only did everything, I could control everything. It isn't that way when you deal with real people and real circumstances.

Every week in camp we formed one or two teams and had them play against each other or against the college teams. On Fridays, we evaluated every player, calling them into the office one at a time. It made for a grueling end of the week, but it had to be done.

We offered some players a Clowns contract. One of them was a tough kid out of Milwaukee, Wisconsin, a catcher named Dave Geis.

Dave came to the Ocala camp three years in a row. He was cut twice, but the third time was the charm and we signed him.

Dave not only developed into a solid player for us, but eventually we took him in as a part owner of the Clowns. He remains a great friend to this day. See, perseverance does pay off.

We gave some other players provisional contracts, putting them on what we called our taxi squad. That made them available to be called up in case of injury or some other development that created a vacancy on the roster. We sent others to Utica.

Most players didn't make either the Clowns or the Blue Sox, though, and we had to release them. It was never pleasant, because you were killing a kid's dream when you sent him home, but most of them took it well. Most of them.

There was one kid, a pitcher named Bernie Tooth, who just would not accept the bad news. Bernie thought he was God's gift to pitching. He had a fastball he thought he could get up there at ninety-five miles an hour, which would have been excellent. But he was kidding himself; the pitch registered only about eighty on the radar gun. And besides, he had no control of his pitches. He could throw all day and never get one over the plate.

We brought Bernie in one afternoon to pitch the fourth inning of one of those camp games. It was blistering hot, with the sun beating down on us from a cloudless blue sky. Bernie must have thrown eighty or ninety pitches. That half-inning went on for forty-five minutes, and all of us on the field were dying of the heat. I was standing out at first base, my uniform soaked through and through and the sweat just pouring off me, until I couldn't take it anymore. Mercifully, we finally got out of the inning.

That Friday, we called Bernie into the office for his evaluation, which wasn't good. We had decided to release him.

"Bernie, you need to move on with your life," I said, giving it to him straight. "You're not going to be a professional pitcher. I know you've got the confidence, but you don't have the skills to match it. You're not being realistic about your chances to succeed in this game."

Bernie got a look in his eyes that was a little scary. I could see something building inside him as I talked.

When I finished, he said in a voice that hissed and rose in pitch and volume: "You're the devil. You're evil. You are *evil.*"

He went on and on like that, telling me what a terrible excuse for a human being I was, and finally I stopped him and said, "Bernie, that all may be true, but you still can't pitch."

He backed toward the door and out of the office, all the while yelling at me, hissing.

"You're the devil! The *devil.*"

Chapter 22:

Two Shows in One

An important part of the Clowns was, well, the clowns.

Finding the right clowns for the job—*our* job—was as difficult as finding the right players. No, it was more difficult. In fact, we signed and released more clowns than players, looking for the ones who would be just the right fit.

We couldn't use just any clown. A circus clown, for example, usually wouldn't do. He might be funny, but chances are he wouldn't know baseball. Our clowns had to know baseball. They had to know when to be out there, being funny, and when to stay in the background. A clown couldn't slow down the game or interfere with play. If he did, he didn't last long.

Our clowns didn't just have to *know* baseball, they had to know how to *play* baseball, and had to do it with some skill. You never knew when you might have to tell a clown to put on a uniform—a Clowns uniform—and go out and play right field for a game or two. That occasionally happened when we found ourselves shorthanded, for one reason or another—maybe injuries or maybe … well, we'll get to that later. The point is, we didn't want a clown out in the field embarrassing himself, or us.

People who came to see the Clowns expected a well-played baseball game and an entertaining and funny show. Giving them both on the same night wasn't easy. We played sixty to eighty games a year, and in the five years we had the team there were maybe ten times when it all came together.

Some nights we played a good game but the clowning flopped. Some nights the clowning was great but the playing was awful. Some nights both the clowning and the playing stunk up the place. We went out every night, though, trying to give people what they came to see. When we thought we had nailed it, it was a great feeling.

The entertainment part we called The Show. Making it work was Sal Tombasco's responsibility. I managed the team, and Mark Anglehart drove the bus and was in charge of transportation. Sal ran The Show.

He usually had two clowns, sometimes three, and he did a lot of clowning himself, under various names, including Alabama Sal and Rocko the Clown. I quickly realized that Sal was as good as any of them when he put his mind to it. The thing is, he wanted to be a baseball player, not a clown. He was a decent baseball player, too, and could play all over the infield—second or third base is where we had him most often. But he was a terrific clown.

I think I've made it clear that I'm an intense guy and always have been. If we're losing a game, any game, it's usually a good idea to leave me alone. It's not likely I'll be in a jovial mood. So I began to realize how funny Sal was when I caught myself laughing at his antics late in games that we were losing. He was that good.

After watching him perform during those five seasons that we owned the Clowns, I'd have to say he's the best baseball clown I've ever seen. And that includes some of the acknowledged great ones, like the Phillie Phanatic and the San Diego Chicken.

Sal gave one of his best clown performances during a game we played in July of 1985 at Doubleday Field in Cooperstown, New York, the home of the Baseball Hall of Fame. Sal was working with two other clowns that day, but he completely stole the show. He had the crowd in stitches. It was the perfect venue for it, too, and the perfect time—Cooperstown, a big crowd, and television's Charles Kuralt on hand with a film crew to do a segment on the Clowns for his "Sunday Morning" show on CBS.

Much of The Show on any given day or night was spontaneous, varying with the mood of the clowns or the mood of the crowd, the response to the opening skits or maybe just the tempo of the game. But some parts were scripted and well rehearsed.

One of the favorite routines of crowds everywhere was something we called Shadow Ball. It was the Clowns' signature routine. Shadow Ball was an infield drill set to music, but with no ball. They'd play "Jump" by Van Halen over the P.A. system, and we'd pretend to toss an imaginary ball around the infield. Each player picked up a handful of dirt before we started the drill, so that when someone "threw" the ball, a puff of dirt would come flying out of his hand. It was very effective, and people loved it.

Sal had a ragdoll umpire that he'd throw out of the dugout after a close play during the game. Then he'd run out of the dugout, jump on the doll and beat on it.

He had a skit that he worked with another clown, where they'd hop on an inflatable raft or a couple of inner tubes and pretend to be rowing a boat, using bats as oars. Sal would pretend to fall out of the boat, and the other clown would rescue him and pretend to be resuscitating him. As the other clown pressed on his chest, Sal would spit out a stream of water.

One night, at Tim McCarver Stadium in Memphis, Tennessee, Sal was doing a popular skit in which he would put a young boy or girl, usually five years old or younger, at home plate between innings and toss a ball from a short distance away. This particular night, Sal called on a little kid who happened to have a very nice swing. I remember being over at first base, throwing grounders to the infielders, and watching this kid take practice swings and thinking, *Sal, you better watch this one.* Then I remember yelling it as Sal let go with a toss: "Sal, you better ..."

WHOPPPP!

There was a crack of the bat and, a split second later, a crack of the skull as a line drive caught Sal between the eyes. Sal's knees buckled and he fell to the ground and lay there, not moving. The kid dropped the bat and started running the bases. Meanwhile, the fans were hysterical, thinking this was all part of the act. But Sal was out cold, and we had to call for a stretcher to carry him off the field. All the while, the kid's still running the bases and the fans are still going wild.

I watched this crazy scene unfolding before me and I thought, *Maybe we should make this part of The Show.*

When I got to the clubhouse, Sal was still lying on the stretcher, but conscious now. He had a nice lump on his forehead that was still growing.

"How you doin', Sal?" I said.

He just groaned.

"Don't worry, you're gonna be okay."

Another groan.

"You know," I said, "that was the best reaction we've gotten from a cro ..."

"Don't even think about it," Sal snapped. "I'm never doing that again."

At some point in every game, just as the Clowns took the field, the announcer would say, "Well, folks, it looks like the pitcher needs relief," and one of the clowns would drag out a toilet that had been attached to a small platform on wheels. The pitcher would sit on the toilet for a bit, and then get this look of relief in his face, and hop back up and start throwing. Almost without fail, the crowd would howl as the toilet was hauled away.

One night I decided to get in the act. Before we went out to the field, I had somebody get a candy bar—a Mounds or a Three Musketeers or something else covered with chocolate—and put it in the toilet. Then, after we did that skit and the pitcher got ready to warm up, I called out from first base, "Hey, wait a minute! Hold on!" I went over to the toilet, lifted the lid, peered in, smiled mischievously at the crowd, and reached in. By now the fans were going nuts. I pulled out this brown block, gave the crowd another crazy grin, and chomped into the chocolate. The ballpark erupted in laugher.

I'm not sure why I decided to do it that night, but it sure worked. I never got the urge to do it again, though, and I never did.

Not all of our clowning ideas worked so well. In our first year as owners, 1984, during one of our first games, we were playing in Daytona Beach, Florida. My cousin Lyle—his real name is Tim Strawser, but everybody calls him Lyle—played a clown called Rainbow, and this day we invited all the kids in the stands to come down onto the field between innings and chase Rainbow around the bases.

About a thousand kids came down, and it was chaos out there for a while. I think maybe all the kids running around on the field got Lyle confused.

The announcer told the kids they were supposed to give chase when Rainbow got halfway to second base, and they were supposed to try to beat him to third. Lyle, who is mentally challenged, understood he was supposed to race the kids, but he got a little carried away when the boys and girls closed in on him.

At around the shortstop position, a boy of about six pulled alongside Lyle and tried to pass him. Lyle elbowed him in the face and sent him sprawling in the dirt. All the other kids ran by this boy, who continued to lie facedown on the base path, until everybody had made it around third. We Clowns all rushed to the boy's aid, and fortunately he was okay except for a little drop of blood on his lip.

In the dugout later, I grabbed Lyle and started yelling at him.

"What the hell were you doing out there?" I screamed. "You could have killed that kid. What's the matter with you?"

"But Dave," he said, "you told me I had to beat them to third."

We had an equipment man named Tank. He was a big, good-natured guy who also was mentally challenged. When I say big, I mean *big*. He stood six-foot-four and weighed three hundred and thirty-one pounds. In a Kmart store once, Sal put him on a scale and weighed him.

Sal described him as "three hundred and thirty-one pounds of joy," and that pretty much says it all.

Tank would do anything for you and, in fact, did just about everything for the Clowns, including sometimes playing a clown and also serving as batboy. He adopted the Clowns as his second family and we adopted him, and he occasionally accompanied us on short road trips.

In Tampa, Florida, one night, we played before an all-black crowd. There were about two thousand fans in the stands, but the only white faces belonged to Mom and Dad and Dad's niece Sandy, who had all come down to visit us. We put Tank in a chicken suit that day, and he went out between innings at one point and, to the surprise of all of us, started doing the Michael Jackson moonwalk down the first-base line. He was terrific, too.

The crowd loved it and started chanting, "Go, Missa Chicken Man … Go, Missa Chicken Man …" Tank fed off the reaction and didn't want to stop. He was holding up the game and we couldn't get him off the field. All the while, the crowd kept chanting. Finally, Sal ran out from the dugout, grabbed Tank and pulled him off the field.

During a game in Valdosta, Georgia, Tank came out of the dugout between innings to pick up the bat our last hitter had left at the plate. At the same time, the Valdosta manager, whose name was Ralph Starling, had come out to coach at third base. He apparently thought the bat at the plate was one of his team's, and he picked it up and started toward his dugout with it. Tank, who had picked up another bat on the way, saw this and started after Ralph.

Our GM/PA announcer, Al Tobin, realized what was happening and called to Tank to stop, but it did no good. Tank kept marching toward Ralph, the bat held menacingly over his head. Down at first base, I heard Al's voice coming from the speakers, looked over to see Tank closing in on Ralph, and yelled to him, "Tank, no! *Stop!*"

For some reason, I always had the ability to get Tank to listen to me and do what I said. When he heard my voice now, he pulled up, looked my way and put the bat down. Ralph came that close to being clubbed senseless.

Lyle and Tank weren't the only ones who could sometimes be difficult. One guy, who went by the name of Tickles the Clown and had worked in the circus, came to me one day and showed me a ball he'd found, which had been autographed, "Lyle, No. 1 Clown." Tickles was offended and wanted me to tell Lyle he couldn't bill himself that way, not even on autographs. See what I mean about circus clowns?

During a game in Jasper, Indiana, in 1988, we were playing before a small crowd, maybe two hundred people. It wasn't much of a game, either, and at some point I suddenly realized I hadn't seen our new clown all night. I called time, went to the mound as if I wanted to talk to Tim Walsh, who was pitching, but I was really interested in finding out from Sal where the clown was.

I motioned Sal to the mound and said, "Where the hell is the clown? Where *is* he? The baseball sucks tonight, there's nobody in the stands, and we've got no show. You're in charge of The Show. Where's the clown?"

Sal told me later I got so mad at him, he thought my eyeballs were going to pop out of my head. But he was no help that night. He didn't know where the clown was anymore than I did.

"Look, let's get through this inning," he said. "Then I'll go find him, honest."

I went back to first base and was so distracted that when the runner over there took a big lead and Tim threw over, I just watched as the ball sailed past me.

When we finally got out of the inning, Sal went looking for the clown and finally found him. The guy was hiding between the seats on the team bus. Sal came and told me.

"What's he doing hiding on the bus?" I said.

"You'll never guess. He's got stage fright."

Some clown *he* was.

CHAPTER 23:

BIG TROUBLE

As a baseball team, the Clowns of that first year, 1984, were the best of the five teams we had. Four of our starting pitchers and our regular catcher had all played pro ball before, some of them as high as Class Double-A—that's just two steps below the major leagues. And there was talent throughout the roster.

I just wish I could have kept that team together for the whole season.

We were in Jasper, Indiana, in late June for a two-game series against the Jasper Reds. I had just come back from a date late that first night when Mark Anglehart told me I ought to check out one of the hotel rooms. He gave me the number.

"What's going on?" I said.

"Just check it, Dave," he said. "You'll see."

I went to the room with Mark and Sal and walked in without knocking. There sat five of my players, playing cards and smoking marijuana. The room reeked of it. For a while, we all just exchanged glances, none of us sure what to say. Three of the players were starting pitchers, and another was our catcher. I honestly can't remember who the fifth player was.

Finally, Sal said, "We've got a problem, Dave."

"There's no problem," I said. "You boys are done. Pack up your things."

They protested, loudly, but I reminded them that they'd all been given the rules in spring training, and the rules stated very clearly that the use of illegal drugs was grounds for dismissal from the Clowns. As much as I hated to break up the team, I really had no choice.

The timing was lousy. Just a week later, we were scheduled to play in Cooperstown, with Charles Kuralt and his CBS crew on hand to film us. Now we needed to fill some big holes in the roster, and quick. This is when you turn to the taxi squad, or anyplace else where you can find, as a quick fix, a body to put in a uniform.

We had one more game in Jasper and then, two days later, a game in Louisville, Kentucky. Then we were to stop at Bluefield, West Virginia, and head home to Corning to play some dates in upstate New York. I got on the phone and called our general manager, Mike Bowers, back in Corning and told him to set up open tryouts there for when we got back.

Meanwhile, we had to make do with what we had. A lot of positions were affected because a couple of the pitchers I had to let go also played other positions when they weren't pitching. All at once, we seemed to have holes everywhere.

We took our public address announcer, who was a former high school pitcher, and had him pitch the next day. Another pitcher filled in at shortstop, and two of the clowns had to play in that game, too. Sal played short in a clown's costume one night, and my cousin Lyle played left field once or twice. An outfielder who also was the backup catcher became our starting catcher.

Going to the park the next night, I was probably more nervous than I've ever been for a game with the Clowns. I thought we'd get killed. As it was, we lost 5–1. But, all things considered, I was satisfied with that.

We moved on to Bluefield, and I was surprised to find us ahead 8–1 going into the eighth inning that night. I felt so good about our lead that I took out our starting pitcher and put Sal in. He occasionally pitched in situations like that—when we were comfortably ahead or hopelessly behind. Sal gave up one run in the eighth, we failed to score in the top of the ninth, and we were three outs away from hitting the road to Corning.

Forty minutes later, it was 8–7, Bluefield had a runner at first and there were two outs. I was beginning to think we'd never get out of there, and I hated myself for changing pitchers. Their next hitter doubled, and the runner from first raced home with the apparent tying run. On the throw home, the batter went to third.

I called time and walked over to the mound from my position at first base.

"We'd like to get out of here some time tonight," I told Sal.

"You think I'm not trying?"

"I know you're trying. But, look, I've got an idea. The guy who was on first barely caught the corner of the bag at second, and I'm not sure if the umpire was even watching. If we appeal, we might get the call. It's worth a try."

Sal gave me a puzzled look. I knew he wasn't sure what to do.

"Just get set on the rubber," I said. "Then back off, call time and throw to second base. Tell the umpire at second you're appealing the runner who was on first. Not the batter, but the runner from first. Got it?"

"Got it," he said, and I went back to my position.

Sal got set on the rubber, backed off, called time and threw to second, then spun around and announced to the umpire—the home plate umpire—"I'm appealing. He missed the bag."

"Which runner?" the ump said.

"That one," Sal said, indicating the guy at third, and I could have killed him.

"He's out!" the ump said, raising his right arm.

At the same time, I was screaming at Sal: "Not him, you idiot! The other guy missed the bag. The runner from first, dammit!"

When he heard me, Sal started babbling to the umpires that he had made a mistake, he meant the runner, not the batter. Really messing it up now. I still wanted to go over there and strangle him.

When the ump made the call, Sal and I weren't sure how to react at first. Sal had screwed up the appeal, but the umpire had at least called an out, and so now we were finally out of the inning and we still had a shot at winning in extras. We accepted the gift without question and went into the dugout while the Bluefield fans, players, manager and coaches went a little crazy.

It seemed the whole team converged on the umpire at the plate, vehemently protesting the call. They had tied the game, but their rally had been snuffed out with the potential winning run at third. Now they all argued that the batter had gotten plenty of second base when he rounded the bag, and, to be honest, they were right. I saw it all.

Then the situation took another sharp turn.

The umps had a conference to discuss the play, which seemed to have caught them off guard—as intended. When they came out of their huddle, they announced that the lead runner was actually the one who was out, and not the batter, and so the tying run did not score.

The game was over, and we had won 8–7.

Now the Bluefield guys really went nuts, and I didn't blame them. Sal had appealed for the wrong runner, the umpires had gotten the call wrong and then had reversed it—wrong again—and we came away with the win. Amazing.

We got the hell out of there while the getting was good.

After an all-night bus ride from Bluefield to Corning, we had that open tryout, looking to replace the players I'd had to let go.

Ten or twelve prospects showed up. We took the best of them and filled the vacant roster spots. One of the players we signed was Dennis Sullivan of nearby Addison, who had been one of that area's top high school pitchers. He turned out to be pretty effective for us and even worked his way into the starting rotation. Dennis and an infielder named Dave Stalbird of Corning stayed with the team for the rest of that season.

Sullivan, a right-hander, began the next season with the Clowns, too. He had really learned how to pitch by then, and he got a tryout with the New York Yankees organization at one point that season. The Clowns had a working agreement with the Yankees, and it was every Clown's dream to get a tryout with New York or some other organization. Very few did, and even fewer were signed by those organizations. But that's why they were with the Clowns—to at least have a shot at moving up.

Charles Kuralt and his TV crew had met us in Corning when we got home from Bluefield. They filmed some of our game the next night, when we played the Wayland Yankees, a team of college players, at the Babe Ruth League field in Corning's Denison Park. The place had no stands and no outfield wall. It was in sharp contrast to Doubleday Field in Cooperstown, where we played the following day.

In Cooperstown, we played the Milford Macs, a semi-pro team from nearby Milford, and they beat us. Harry Hillson was a player-coach for Milford. He later became one of the nation's top Division II baseball coaches at Mansfield University in Pennsylvania.

Kuralt did a nice job with the "Sunday Morning" segment on the team. He and the crew had taken the bus ride from Corning to Cooperstown with us, and had done some interviews on the bus. They had lots of film from the games and our practices, too. It made for a package that we felt fairly and accurately depicted the life of the Indianapolis Clowns. We were proud to have been on his program.

CHAPTER 24:

BLACK AND WHITE

After the second or third game during our first year as owners of the Clowns, our bus broke down on the way back to Ocala from Jacksonville. As we would learn, this was not an unusual occurrence, but it was particularly inconvenient this time. We were in the middle of the Ocala National Forest in the dead of night, stranded on an isolated stretch of highway miles from the closest source of assistance.

I got out of the bus and stuck out my thumb and hitchhiked to Ocala, a distance of about forty miles. Some guy was good enough to pick me up and drop me off at a gas station, where I was able to get somebody to drive out and look at the bus.

It wasn't until later that I found out the Ocala National Forest is a favorite dumping ground for serial killers. It's where they like to stash the bodies, I was told, because the region is so remote for such a long distance. When I heard that, I thought, *Damn, how crazy was I to be thumbing a ride out there?* And how crazy was the guy who picked me up? Maybe he hadn't heard about the dumping ground either.

That wasn't the worst of it, though. Not by a long shot. Heck, I'd rather take my chances with a serial killer than with some of the people we really had to deal with.

The Clowns always carried a number of black players on the roster. After all, this was a team that been proud to put a uniform on Satchel Paige and Hank Aaron, among other outstanding African-Americans.

Besides, all of baseball was integrated now. Every team wanted the best players it could get, regardless of color. So it wasn't unusual that we had a black player named Bobo "Lefty" Smalls on the team in 1985. Lefty was our headline clown at the time, and a pitcher, and he'd been at it for a long time—he was pitching for the Clowns when I first played for them. Bobo had such huge hands, he could hold five baseballs at one time and throw them, in one motion, to five catchers stationed around home plate. And hit every one of them, too. You had to see it to believe it.

We had Bobo with us when we checked into a motel in Atlanta, Georgia, one night and got everybody assigned to rooms. It was an okay place—from a national chain, but one in the economy class. We were going to be playing in the area for a week, so we were basically setting up a base of operations. It would be good to have the same place to come home to every night, even if only for several days.

We'd played an afternoon game that day and arrived at the motel at around ten at night. After we checked in, and paid for a week in advance, Sal and I went straight to our room and then I headed for the shower. It felt so good to soak in the steaming water, I just let it lull me nearly to sleep standing there. Suddenly there was a pounding at the door. Sal opened up and I heard a woman's voice screaming and yelling.

The voice kept getting closer and louder, and pretty soon somebody pushed open the shower door and I was standing there, stark naked and dripping wet, looking into the flushed face of the motel manager. She was a woman. The same woman, in fact, who just minutes before had checked us into the place.

"I'm kicking you guys out of here," she yelled at me.

"What?"

"You gotta go. That nigger's nothing but trouble."

That's a word I can't stand, that n-word. I've worked and played with people of all races all my life, and I've never been able to put up with people talking like that. When I think about it, I trace it back to when I was a kid and our family was on a vacation trip and we stopped at a restaurant for lunch. We ordered, and a black couple came in a little later and sat at another table. The waitress wouldn't serve them and told them they had to leave. They just got up and walked outside. Dad watched them go and said, "If they can't eat here, then we won't either," and he took us all out of there. I've never forgotten that.

Now I told the motel manager, "Lady, if you would have enough respect to back your ass out of my bathroom, I'll dry off and come talk to you. But not until then."

Reluctantly, she left the room.

When I had toweled myself dry, I threw on a robe and went out to the bedroom and found the woman waiting for me, no less furious than before.

"That nigger got disrespectful to me," she yelled. "And now you boys are gonna have to get out of here."

"What did he do?" I said.

"You heard what I said. Now, come on, git, all of ya, or I'll have the whole bunch of ya arrested."

She went on and on, and while she was yelling, four or five Georgia state patrol cars pulled up out front and a bunch of troopers spilled out of them. The one in charge was a big, fat guy who looked like the Jackie Gleason character from those "Smokey and the Bandit" movies. He came waddling up to the door and said, "You boys are gonna have to get out of here, or we're gonna string up that nigger."

That didn't leave us much choice. And by this time I really didn't want to stay in that place anyway. We rounded up the guys and climbed back on the bus. Before we rolled out, I took a head count. We were one short. Bobo.

We pulled out anyway, figuring Bobo must have split when he heard the ruckus. The bus turned left and headed down a road that was lined with hedges on our right. We had the windows and the door open, and as we started off slowly down the block I heard a *psst* sound coming from somewhere. I called for Mark to slow down even more, and when he did, there it was again—a little louder and more urgent this time. *Psssst!*

Somebody said, "What's that? We got a leak in the tire?"

"I don't think so," I said, but I couldn't tell for sure. We all kept quiet, and kept listening. The traffic light at the corner was red, and we pulled up to it and stopped.

Just then, somebody came flying out of the hedges and dived head-first onto the bus. I said, "Bobo, where the hell have you been?"

He'd been hiding in the hedges, just waiting for an opportunity to hop on the bus. I don't know what he'd have done if that light hadn't changed.

I talked to Bobo about what had happened at the motel and asked if he'd done anything to offend the woman. He said all he'd done was go to the office looking for some towels. I'd already asked a few of the other players, and they'd told me the same thing.

Later, I wrote to the motel chain and told them about our experience at one of their fine establishments in Atlanta. I got a reply some time later, apologizing for the treatment we'd received and letting me know the manager of that motel had been fired. It made me feel a little better, but not much.

We never did get a refund.

Looking back, we had mostly good experiences in motels, though. Usually, we were so happy to get to one that we didn't care much what it looked like, or whether it had a pool or any other extra conveniences or attractions. We'd generally roll into the parking lot so tired we just wanted a mattress we could fall onto. We'd usually have played a game the evening before and then rocked and bounced on the bus for a few hours, or most of the night, or sometimes all of it. Everybody complained if we had to sleep on the bus, even if it was only parked in a lot somewhere. We just wanted to get out of there, maybe get a shower and then sleep on a real mattress for as long as we could.

One morning, Mark drove us into the parking lot of a motel in Rockmart, Georgia, just before daylight after an all-night ride. It was nothing special, just an old, rundown mom-and-pop place that sat beside the road, looking about as beat as we felt. Sal and I went into the office and found a fat old black woman behind the desk.

"Got any rooms?" I said. "We've got a busload of ballplayers."

"Got lots of rooms," she said.

"How much you asking?"

"Fifteen dollars a night."

Sal and I decided that wasn't too bad, and asked to see one of them.

"Follow me," she said, and led us to the room next to the office. She inserted a key, opened the door and stepped aside. "Let me know," she said, and went back to the office.

Sal and I stuck our heads inside, and a foul odor backed us out just as fast.

"Wow, something died in here," Sal said.

"It does smell a bit, doesn't it?"

"A bit? I've got dirty socks smell better than this place."

"Still …" I said.

"Yeah, I know. We're all tired as hell."

So we took it. When we got into our rooms, we found mattresses with no sheets or blankets, pillows with no pillow cases, and bugs flying and crawling everywhere.

We must have been more tired than I remember, because we plopped down on the beds anyway and fell dead asleep, every one of us.

When I finally woke up, I felt a mist falling on my face. I figured Sal was up to something so I just tried to ignore it, but it continued. I swiped at it, whatever it was, still not bothering to open my eyes, still fighting to go back to sleep. The mist persisted. Eventually, I opened my eyes, looked up and saw a huge hole in the roof. And it was raining.

Pretty soon players started knocking on our door. They'd all had similar experiences and wanted to complain to us. One of them had slept in his skivvies and was covered with bug bites from head to toe.

We had a game that day, and another in the area the next night, so we'd paid for two nights in advance. The second night the whole team piled into the bus and we slept there in the parking lot. And nobody complained.

CHAPTER 25:

WORST GAME EVER

When I started playing again in 1984, something unusual happened: I had to bat.

I hadn't batted since 1975, when I first played for the Clowns. All organized baseball leagues, except for the National League, had been using the designated hitter since 1973, so as a pitcher I'd always had a DH to bat for me. But with the Clowns, it was different. I was playing first base now. Position players everywhere were expected to bat.

Usually, I wasn't expected to run, though. And that was a good thing because, with the crutches and the leg brace, I couldn't get down the baseline nearly as fast as your average runner, or even a slow one. Most of the teams we played had no problem with us using a designated runner, or courtesy runner as it was called. Occasionally, though, the opposing team would object, and I'd have to run the bases.

When I had a courtesy runner, he was always stationed behind the umpire and catcher, to the third base side of home plate—behind me, too, because I hit right-handed. He wasn't allowed to start running until my bat made contact with the ball. If he left early, it was an automatic out.

I was never a great hitter, but I could handle a bat pretty well. For Hunnewell in 1972, I batted twenty-eight times and had seven hits, for a .250 average. That's not too shabby for a pitcher.

In 1984, I hit .159 for the Clowns, with thirteen hits in eighty-two at-bats. The arm injury affected my swing and cut down on what little power I had. But I was determined to fight through the pain and make myself a better hitter. I'd take a bat, stand in front of a full-length mirror and swing a hundred times a day. I kept taking extra swings in the cage every day all season, and I continued it every year I played after that.

My batting average kept improving. My second year with the Clowns, I hit .257, with twenty-eight hits in a hundred and nine at-bats. The next year, I hit .266, with twenty-five hits in ninety-four at-bats. And in 1987, I broke .300 for the first time, bating .301, with thirty-seven hits in a hundred and twenty-three times up. I drove in twelve runs that year, too, and that was my career high.

I was badly injured that first season with the Clowns, but I missed only three weeks because of it. I broke my right ankle during a game in DeMoines, Iowa, on a kind of freak play. There was a throw from shortstop or third base, I can't remember which, and it short-hopped me. I was a good fielder and could usually pick those, but this one hit the dirt just in front of me and skidded under my glove. It hit me flush on the ankle bone, and I crumpled to the ground. Right away, I knew I was in trouble, but I tried to shake it off and stayed at my position for the rest of the inning.

After the last out of the inning, I hobbled to the dugout in terrible pain. I couldn't put any weight on the right leg, and when I got into the dugout I realized I couldn't move the ankle at all. Somebody called an ambulance, and I got a ride to the hospital.

It turned out to be a bad break. The doctors re-set the bone and put my leg in a cast that covered me from my toes to the knee.

When I finally got back to the hotel, I went to my room and tried to take a bath. That experience would have been funny if it hadn't been excruciatingly painful. I ran some hot water, stretched out in the tub and propped my right leg on the edge. They'd given me some painkillers at the hospital, but I've never liked to take drugs of any kind, so I just put up with it and got washed up as quickly as possible.

I flew home to Corning the next day. In the process, I saw a good bit of the U.S.A., at least from the air, traveling from DeMoines to

Denver, to Kansas City (Missouri), to Detroit and, finally, to Rochester, New York. My parents met me there and drove me home.

About two weeks later, I went to see Doug Frey, the head of the sports rehab unit at St. Joseph's Hospital in Elmira. Doug had helped me when I was rehabbing my arm. Now I wanted him to take a look at the ankle. More than that, I wanted him to cut the cast off. The Clowns were due back in the area in five days, and I intended to rejoin them then.

Doug cut the cast off but made no promises to keep it off.

"I need to see what's going on here," he said. "I'll have to take some pictures."

They X-rayed me, and Doug wasn't happy with what he saw. He explained to me what had happened to the bone and what was happening now as it began to heal. And he gave me some idea of what would happen next. All of which I dismissed as quickly as I heard it.

"I need you to fit me with something smaller," I said. "Something I can get a shoe over. I can't play in this."

"Play?" he said. "You can't play on this ankle, Dave, not for a good while yet. If you want my opinion ..."

"I don't," I said. "Just fit it."

He put a much smaller cast on. It covered only the ankle itself, which was just what I wanted. I could put a shoe on again. I could stand on the foot. I could play with this cast, even if Doug didn't think I could and didn't want me to. He didn't, and again he warned me against it.

I met the Clowns when they came back to Corning, and I put on a uniform again. It felt good. Then I put myself back in the lineup. Three weeks after breaking the ankle, I was back out on the field, playing baseball.

About five weeks later, Doug checked out the ankle again. This time, he cut the small cast off and I was as good as new.

I made it through that first Clowns season by smoke and mirrors. If the arm injury affected my hitting, it was even more of a problem in the field. Even at first base, throwing was a problem for me, and I tried to disguise the fact as best I could.

When I threw the ball around the infield between innings, I always lobbed it to shortstop and third base, and tired to appear nonchalant while doing so, as if I was only being lazy. If I took a pickoff throw from the pitcher, I'd quickly grab the ball out of my glove and snap it back to the pitcher with a wrist motion. I found I could do that from that distance without really using the arm. Sometimes, if the play called for me to make a strong throw, I'd fake tripping or slipping to avoid having to get rid of the ball at all. Not very ingenious stuff, maybe, but it worked.

After the season, I saw my doctor back home and he told me I'd probably need surgery on the arm. He suggested I see a specialist, so I went back to Scott Teets, the Orioles team doctor, and asked if he could recommend someone. He sent me to Doctor James Andrews, who had gained fame operating on some of the big-name pitchers in baseball, as well as athletes in other sports. I was fortunate to have him see me.

Doctor Andrews practiced in Columbus, Georgia, at the time, and after I made an appointment I drove down with Dad that October for an exam and a consultation. Doctor Andrews performed the surgery the next morning, and the following day he had me out in the hospital yard, lobbing a baseball. It was that quick.

I wasn't throwing, but I was lobbing without pain, and I had my range of motion back. For the first time in a long while, I was able to comb my hair, eat and do other daily chores with no pain.

I wasn't going to start pitching again, but I felt I could play at my best again. That was a wonderful feeling.

The worst team of the five we had as owners of the Clowns was the club we had in 1985, our second year.

The first season we had to deal with the players we caught smoking marijuana—their release and the problems that followed. The second year we got a letter from the NCAA two days before the season opener. It notified us that six of our players still had college eligibility, and that they would lose it if they played for us. Sal and Mark and I met with those players the next day and laid it out for them—they could stay with the Clowns and lose their eligibility, or they could leave now.

They left, all six of them.

We called up some players from the taxi squad, but they didn't fill our needs. We tried out others and signed some of them, but they still weren't as good as the ones we'd lost. All season, we had a revolving door on the clubhouse, bringing in and sending out players on a regular basis. We never really recovered from the loss of those college kids that whole season.

The worst game I ever played was witnessed by a sellout crowd one night in Eau Claire, Wisconsin, in 1987. The Clowns as a team played just awful that night, and I was a big part of it. I booted two routine grounders at first base on balls that barely made it into the outfield. Most nights, I could have made those plays in my sleep. This night, I played as if I *was* asleep.

We were behind 6–0 after one inning and 12–0 after two. We went on to lose 27–4. It was the worst loss I can ever remember being a part of.

After the game, I couldn't wait to get off the field. I was the first one in the clubhouse, and I proceeded to take one of my aluminum crutches and smash it against a steel post that stood in the middle of the room. I hammered it over and over and over. When I was finished, the crutch was bent way out of shape, and I was still bent out of shape myself.

After a while, Sal Tombasco came in from outside and walked over to where I was sulking.

"Look, Dave, I know you're upset," he said, "but there's a little girl outside in a wheelchair waiting to get your autograph."

That got to me. Immediately, it seemed to drain all the anger out of me.

"Help me with this, will ya?" I said, handing Sal the mangled crutch.

Sal took it, put it on the floor and jumped up and down on it a few times. When it was straight enough that I could use it again, I took it and hobbled outside, where I found a girl of ten or twelve sitting patiently in a wheelchair near the clubhouse door. A man who was with her identified himself as her father.

"She thinks what you did tonight was absolutely terrific," he said.

"Ah, I was awful," I said. "That was the worst game I've ever played in my life. I'm sorry you had to see it. To tell you the truth, I'm just embarrassed about what happened out there."

The girl said, "There's no need to feel embarrassed. You were great. Just to be out there competing with those other guys, that was unbelievable."

Well, that was just what I needed right then. That put things in perspective for me and changed my perception of myself. The little girl was right: Just being on the field with so-called able-bodied athletes and competing with them was a victory in itself. I needed to be reminded of that.

I've never forgotten what that girl said to me that night. I wish I could thank her. Since then, whenever I've felt the urge to blow my top, I've tried to think of her and what she said, and I've often used that experience to get myself under control. I'm still the same competitive guy, and I still sometimes let my temper get the best of me, but that little girl taught me to appreciate all that I've accomplished.

After hitting .301 in 1987, I was looking forward to another good season. The team was doing well, I was playing some of my best baseball, and I was eager to get back at it. I kept working on my swing that off-season, hoping I could pull the batting average even higher and maybe knock in a few more runs in '88.

I could not have dreamed what that year would bring.

CHAPTER 26:

POLIO REVISITED

After any season, I always took off whatever was left of the month of September. Then, starting the first of October, I'd begin my off-season workout routine—four hours a day, six days a week.

I did everything: weights, sprints, distance running, push-ups, pull-ups, the stationary bike, and lots of stretching before and after. Every day, I did four hundred sit-ups, swung the bat twenty-five times, and did other exercises with a bat.

I'd spend three hours at the Corning YMCA, then drive to my parents' house, where they had some free weights and other equipment, and finish my workout there. I liked to start early in the morning, usually around eight o'clock but sometimes as early as six.

It was a tough routine, but it was not taxing at all. I was in good shape, and rather than wear me down, the workouts only energized me.

Until the fall of 1987, that is. From the first day of my off-season workouts that year, something was not right and I could feel it. I didn't know what it was, but all at once it felt like I was running with a weight tied behind me. Fatigue overwhelmed me. I had no energy, I was weak and I ached all over.

At first, I thought maybe I was coming down with the flu. I went home after that first workout and went straight to bed. But I refused to give in to it, whatever it was, and day after day I kept getting up early and going to the gym. And every day I would go home feeling worse, and I'd fall right back into bed.

After a week or so, I realized I didn't have the flu but I knew I had a problem. I went to my doctor, and he seemed as puzzled as I was. He put me through a battery of tests for everything you can imagine, and some things you don't even want to imagine—HIV, tuberculosis, cancer, everything. The results all came back negative.

The prognosis: I was as healthy as a horse. Maybe that should have made me feel better, but it only made me feel worse. I knew what I didn't have—at least if you could believe the test results—but I still didn't know what I had, and I had *something*.

I kept a record of my workouts. On November 5, I revised my schedule and wrote on the sheet, "Change workout due to extreme exhaustion ... Also, shoulder sore again." Now I was lifting weights only on Mondays, running on Thursdays and doing a variety of exercises—sit-ups, pull-ups, stretching and bat swinging, for example—every day.

A week and a half later, I revised the schedule again. I cut out the running and did free weights on Mondays and Fridays, and Universal and Nautilus weights on Wednesdays. That didn't help any. I wasn't getting stronger; I was just getting weaker.

It got to the point where I couldn't carry a bag of groceries from the car into the house. Still, I pushed myself through my daily workouts. I had to keep in shape, no matter what. I had to be ready to play ball again, come spring. That's what drove me.

Finally, I went to Baltimore again to see Scott Teets, the Orioles team doctor who always seemed to be able to help me. He looked me over, felt here and there, pressing, probing. He stood behind me, poked around my shoulder blade area and said, "What's this?"

Now, you never want to hear your doctor or your mechanic say, "What's this?"

"What's what?" I said.

He poked around some more, on the right side.

"Have you been having any pain back here?"

"Oh, that," I said. "I separated my shoulder diving for a ball this season."

I'd almost forgotten. The injury never even kept me out of the lineup. I would just get the shoulder taped up before each game, and keep playing.

Scott told me that what he'd found was a huge pit in my back, around the shoulder blade, where there used to be muscle. Somehow, the muscle had disappeared. It was just gone.

We were both silent for a while as I tried to comprehend what he'd just said. Then Scott asked, "Have you ever heard of post-polio?" I told him I hadn't.

He said post-polio syndrome was a condition that had only recently been identified. It affected people who'd had polio early in life—people like me. He admitted he was no expert in the field, and he thought I ought to see one, so he sent me to Johns Hopkins Medical Center, also in Baltimore, where there *were* experts.

"Listen," Scott said before I left, "I'm really sorry."

"Sorry? For what?"

"For pushing you when you first came to see me. If I'd known about post-polio, I'd have never made you work so hard to get your arm back in condition."

"Hey, there's nothing to be sorry about," I said. "You helped me when nobody else could. You fixed me up. Don't feel bad now that this has happened. It's not your fault.

"Besides," I said, "you know you couldn't have stopped me anyway."

"Still …"

"Forget it. I've had a good run. If this is the price I have to pay, so be it."

At Johns Hopkins, I was given an EMG, which is a series of tests that check the responsiveness of nerves. I'm deathly afraid of needles, and this exam involved inserting two long, thin needles into the muscles all over my body, and then sending electronic signals through the needles. This was done directly into the biceps, the forceps, the neck, shoulders, everywhere.

The test took at least an hour. It confirmed that I had post-polio.

The doctors explained that as people who have had polio get into middle age, their bodies begin wearing down from years of overexertion—shoulder muscles from the constant use of crutches, for example. The polio that we thought we had put behind us, or at least had learned to live with, still had a hold on us, it seemed. It came at us now, after all these years, with a new series of health issues.

I learned that some of our muscles probably were doing ten times the work of other people's muscles. And that was just for people in typical walks of life. As an athlete, I was doing damage to my muscles at a much faster rate. The regular sprinting, the diving for balls, the pitching—all these things were beating up my body.

Okay, so now what?

They gave me one piece of advice: Cut back on my activity.

And just how do you do that? For somebody who's always been very active, what does "cut back" mean? How much is too much? How much is okay? What are the activities I needed to avoid altogether? And which ones could I still do, at least on a limited basis?

Nobody seemed to know.

Now I understood that the end of my playing career was near. In fact, it probably should have ended with that diagnosis. But I didn't want to go out that way. I wanted to play my final season knowing that it would be my last. I wanted to go out on my terms, and so I decided I would.

I told myself I'd cut back on my daily workouts. That's what "cut back" would mean for me—still working out every day, but not as hard. I'd spend something less than four hours a day in the gym for what was left of the off-season. I'd keep myself in shape, though, and I'd play one more season for the Clowns.

And then I'd retire.

Chapter 27:

Playing Days Are Done

The Clowns were going through an infield drill one sunny day that spring in Ocala, Florida. I was fielding grounders at first base when one of them rolled past my outstretched glove and into right field as I tumbled to the dirt.

If I still had any doubts, I realized right then I couldn't kid myself about it: This really would be my last season.

I struggled to my feet, well aware that the young ballplayer I once was would have hopped up and been in position for another grounder by now. Then I walked off down the right-field line, ignoring everyone around me, alone in my thoughts, a cowboy riding off into the sunset.

Later, alone in my car, I sat and played my career over in my mind and let the tears come. It had been a good ride, but now I was heading into the homestretch. I hadn't reached my ultimate dream of playing in the major leagues, but I had accomplished far more than anyone I met along the way ever imagined I would. And I had overcome so much—not just the effects of the polio, the need for full-length leg braces and crutches, but also the injuries and that last arm injury that ended my pitching career.

That day I came to realize that my life was soon going to change, and drastically. After this final season, I would never play again. I just wondered if I had enough left even for one more season. Could I get through those games, the practices, the travel, all of it? I was not sure, but I was determined to give it my best shot.

I had cut back my workouts to about three hours a day. This enabled me to do some stretching, a few reps with weights, and four miles of running instead of my usual six.

I made one other concession to my condition: I let Sal take over as manager of the Clowns. He really seemed to enjoy it, and he did a good job, too.

There was nothing wrong with my hitting, at least through much of the season. I was batting .330 in July, helping us get off to a 25–6 start, the best under our ownership of the team. Then, one afternoon in Nashville, Tennessee, I had to take myself out of a game after what had to be the worst-looking at-bat of my career.

It was a Sunday afternoon following a Saturday night game and then a long bus ride. I thought I was just tired, but it was more than that. We were in the field in the first inning when I started to see spots before my eyes. I tried to shake them out and rub them out, but nothing worked. I couldn't focus on anything, I couldn't pick up the ball, and I was just praying that it wouldn't be hit at me.

Fortunately, nobody did hit to me, but there was a grounder to our second baseman, and I had to take his throw to first. Somehow, I caught the ball.

The next inning, I was due to hit. I sat on the bench for a while, still trying to clear my eyes. Finally, I it was time for me to take a bat and move out to the on-deck circle. And then I was up.

I dug in, looked out at the pitcher and prayed again—this time, that there wouldn't be any inside pitches. I was hoping for four that were outside and low, or high—anything that I wouldn't have to swing at. No such luck. I never got the bat off my shoulder and I struck out looking, which is something I almost never did.

I dragged myself back to the dugout, my head hung low, not wanting to look at anybody. Then I put my bat in the rack and slumped down on the bench.

Sal came over, and I said, "Take me out, Sal. I can't even see the ball. Something's wrong."

The next day, the spots were gone. I felt a lot better—more rested, and ready to play again. We were in Madisonville, Kentucky, now, and as we piled out of the team bus and into the dugout, I got a look at the lineup and noticed my name wasn't there.

"What gives?" I said to Sal. "I'm good to go. Put me in, Coach."

"Not tonight, Dave," Sal said. "Sit this one out. You could use the rest."

Well, he was the manager. It was his call. So I sat that one out. I didn't like it, but I did it.

I wasn't used to just sitting and watching our games. In three seasons with the Clowns—about two hundred games in all—I hadn't missed a game, except for the three weeks after I broke my ankle. And I nearly didn't miss the one at Madisonville—not all of it, anyway.

In the ninth inning, Sal came over to where I was sitting on the bench and plopped down next to me.

"How you feelin', buddy?" he asked.

"Feelin' fine," I said. "Told you that."

"Feel good enough to hit if you have to?"

"Just point the way," I said eagerly.

I was to go in as a pinch-hitter, but I got only as far as the on-deck circle. There were two outs, and the batter ahead of me struck out to end the game.

I never did find out what caused the spots. But a lot of things bothered me that season. Normally, I'm a fast healer, but I wasn't getting over injuries as fast as usual now. I got hit on the hand with a pitch one night, and it bothered me for weeks. I felt run-down most of the summer, with a variety of little things nagging at me all the time.

An athlete gets used to pushing through injuries and illnesses. And my whole life, if something was too tough to tackle, I tackled it. But now I had to back off from time to time, giving my body time to rest and heal. It took me a while to accept that I had to do that.

By the end of the season, I knew I was done. Sal and I used to kid each other about wanting to play until we were fifty, but that wasn't something I could even joke about anymore. I was finished as a player, and Sal had decided to retire, too.

One day that summer, the Corning paper ran an article announcing our plans to end our careers and sell the Clowns franchise. It quoted

Sal as saying: "I didn't want to go on with this team without my partner. We started this thing together, and we said we'd end it together. It'd be nice to continue, but you can see each other's abilities fading."

We never did find a buyer for the team. Technically, we still own the Clowns.

We closed out that 1988 season in Charlotte, North Carolina, on August 14, losing 4–1 to the Charlotte Knights. That's one score I'll never forget.

It wasn't until fifteen years later that I learned of the Indianapolis Clowns' connection to the Negro Leagues. I was contacted by a man named Layton Revel, from Dallas, Texas, who owns a museum dedicated to the Negro Leagues and who was putting together a traveling exhibit featuring Negro League memorabilia.

"The Indianapolis Clowns is the final chapter of Negro League baseball in America," Revel was quoted later in an article about the Clowns in the Elmira newspaper, the Star-Gazette.

Several years after we put the Clowns to rest, a New York City writer named Mark Ribowsky wrote a book called "A Complete History of the Negro Leagues," in which he slandered me and wrote some awful stuff without ever having talked with any of us from that final ownership group. In the book, Ribowsky claims I tried to market the Clowns as black and even sent team photos to newspapers "with black faces pasted on the white players' bodies." He made some other disparaging remarks about the way we handled the team in those final years, none of which he attributes to any source. And, of course, he had no first-hand knowledge.

His claims are absurd. The truth is, the Clowns were mostly white long before we bought the team, and we had few blacks playing for us. Not that we wouldn't have welcomed more—we just took the best players and clowns we could find. But we never marketed the team as black, and nobody who knows anything about the team will tell you otherwise.

When I read that garbage in Ribowsky's book, I wrote him a four-page letter letting off some steam, and I also wrote to his publisher and tried to set the record straight. It was a waste of time.

Ribowsky wrote back, saying he had a source for the Clowns reference, whom he did not identify. But he conceded that he might have made a mistake. Still, he refused to apologize.

Well, that's fine. He's shown his true character. If the rest of his book is as reliable as the part about the Clowns, well, let's just say I wouldn't recommend it. Ribowsky simply made up nonsense to discredit a team that, in its day, was something special. Those of us who were privileged to have been part of the Clowns, in whatever capacity, know that we served it well. Besides, I'd rather take the word of people who I consider better authorities than Ribowsky.

Layton Revel, the founder of the non-profit Center for Negro League Baseball Research, had this to say about the Clowns: "What they have accomplished has had a tremendous amount of importance."

And Prentice Mills, an authority on black baseball, wrote this for the Negro Leagues Baseball Online Archives: "If this is a legacy of which the Clowns alumni are now to be ashamed, it is difficult to imagine a legacy of which one can be proud."

The Clowns were ahead of their time. Look at all the team mascots cavorting around major-league ballparks these days. Take in a minor-league game and check out all the between-innings entertainment that goes on. Decades earlier, the Clowns were doing all that and more. And better, too, if you ask me.

I'm proud of my association with the Clowns. I'm proud of the role, however insignificant, I played in the final days of that final link to the Negro Leagues. And I'm proud to say I ended my playing days when the Clowns organization ended its days.

When I *did* end my playing days, it was time for me to move on with my life.

CHAPTER 28:

MANAGING A NEW LIFE

That fall, November 25 through December 5 of 1988, I took the trip to Canada that was supposed to help me forget about baseball, at least for a little while. It was ten days of watching hockey, plus one football game.

This was one of the lowest points of my life. I thought I had reached rock-bottom when I realized I could no longer pitch, but this was worse. Now I could no longer play, period.

I was down both mentally and physically. Playing baseball was something I had done almost all my life, and something that was so central to my life that—at that point, at least—I could not picture life without it. But I was going to have to start picturing it, and living it, because post-polio syndrome was with me now just as surely as polio had been with me as an infant. There was no way I was ever going to play again.

I began to seriously wonder now if this was the beginning of the end of my life, as well as my career. I ached everywhere, I looked and felt old, and I seemed to have lost the fighting spirit that had always been a part of me. At that point, I could not see myself having the time to find a woman to love and to build a family with, never mind getting a "real" job.

Long after the trip, I continued writing in the journal that I had started in a green spiral notebook when I headed off for Canada.

Reading it over now, I see that my physical and mental condition did not improve much for at least a few months. Here's an excerpt from my entry of March 2, written at one forty-five in the morning:

"It's terrible when you can't tell if you feel lousy because it's a cold or the flu or because of post-polio. And I can't decide whether exercise is actually helping my situation now or hindering. It would be extremely tough for me to stop exercising as it's been such a big part of my life for so long.... It's ironic—exercise and hard work is what got me to the top in sports but now it might be what's tearing me down."

And this, from the same entry: "I'm not quitting. I've never quit on anything in my life. But this post-polio I have no control over, and it's a tough enemy. Seems to be sapping the very life out of me—the enjoyment and satisfaction (they've been diminished). I don't look forward to things as much anymore."

I didn't know much about post-polio back then and, to be honest, I don't know a whole lot more about it now. Most of what I know came from groups like the Steuben Area Post-Polio Support Group back home in Steuben County, New York, and larger organizations like the International Post-Polio Network and the International Post-Polio Task Force. Briefly, here's what I've learned:

As of about midway through the first decade of the 2000s, there were an estimated six hundred thousand polio survivors in the United States and about twenty million worldwide who were experiencing what might be called a second wave of the disease—"a cruel twist of fate," as Samuel Pfaff, an assistant professor at The Salk Institute for Biological Studies, wrote in the May 1990 issue of the Polio Post News. Pfaff explained that polio starts in the motor neurons, the nerves that drive muscles, and he wrote that they are connected to each other by axons, which are long, thin tentacles carrying weak electrical signals.

"It's generally believed," he wrote, "that post-polio syndrome results when these overly extended motor neurons start wearing down over time, the result of metabolic exhaustion."

I guess that means we just over-work them. That's certainly been true in my case.

Even early in the twenty-first century, though, we know little about post-polio, and nothing about how to combat or reverse it, if that's even possible. But the International Post-Polio Task Force, based in Englewood, New Jersey, did a good job of describing its "unexpected and often disabling" symptoms in a newsletter. It listed "overwhelming fatigue; muscle weakness; muscle and joint pain; sleep disorders; heightened sensitivity to anesthesia, cold and pain; and difficulty swallowing and breathing." I can't speak about the sensitivity to anesthesia, but the rest of it described my condition pretty well. The article said the symptoms typically develop thirty-five years after the attack of the polio virus; again, that was right on the nose in my case.

What needs to be understood is that all of this came as quite a shock to a generation of people who had learned to deal with their polio and had moved on with their lives. We had no warning that some day we would experience any of this. If we'd had a warning, I wonder how many of us would have lived our lives differently. I can't say that I would have.

Somehow, I got through that winter. When spring came again to upstate New York in 1989, I got the urge to play ball again, but this time I just had to let it burn itself out. There was nothing I could do to satisfy it.

I had a strong desire to stay in the game somehow, though, and the opportunity came when a friend named Al Goldis called one day with an offer. When I was with the Clowns, Al coached a strong collegiate team on Long Island, and we played them one year. Al and I became close and kept in touch over the years, and he was calling now to ask if I'd be interested in scouting. He was with the Chicago White Sox and was looking for a scout in our region. I took the job and scouted that summer and held tryout camps in Syracuse and Buffalo.

That same year, Sal Tombasco and I started a youth baseball camp in Corning, which we continued operating each summer for a few years. In 1991, two years after we started the camp, we added another camp for kids with disabilities. That one, the Southern Tier Physically and Mentally Disabled Baseball Camp, also in Corning, was very well received. We continued doing it, year after year, and it continues today.

In the fall of 1989, I got a call from Sweden that would start my life down a new and unexpected path. Out of the blue, Magnus Hoglund, a member of the board of directors of the Rattvik Bets, called to ask what I was doing now and if I would be interested in managing the Bets in 1990. Magnus had been a player for the Bets when I first went over to Rattvik as a player, and now, eight years later, he was still playing, in addition to being on the board of directors. His call caught me completely off guard.

At first I told him I really didn't think I wanted to go back to Sweden, and I didn't think I'd be interested in managing, either. I had no aspirations to coach or manage, beyond what I'd done with the Clowns, and I told him so. Magnus said he really wanted me, though, and he tried hard to talk me into it.

"Tell you what," I said finally. "Give me some time to think about it. That's the best I can do for now."

"Take all the time you want," he said. "I'll call you back in three weeks."

For a week or so, I didn't really give it any thought. Then I began to realize this might be a real opportunity. Maybe I *could* start a new career in baseball. Scouting was fine, but being a member of a team, putting on a uniform and getting into the dugout, winning and, yes, even losing—those were things I missed a great deal, and things I could have again as a manager.

I was organized, I was a leader, and I was a lifetime baseball guy. Why *couldn't* I manage? I asked myself the question, finally, and decided the answer was that I could, I sure could. Besides, what else was I going to do with the rest of my life?

When Magnus Hoglund called again three weeks later, I told him I'd take the job, but just for one season. Sal and I had already made plans to start the camp for disabled kids the following year, and that was important enough to me that I was going to go ahead with it, no matter what.

As it turned out, taking the job in Sweden was one of the most important decisions I've ever made. Becoming manager of the Bets was the springboard to everything that followed. It got me into managing and coaching, which included a few seasons with the Swedish Junior National Team and one summer with the U.S. Olympic baseball team. And it led to my becoming a roving scout and instructor for Major League Baseball International.

There's nothing like being a player but, to be honest, I became a bigger name and had a bigger impact on the game as a manager and coach than I ever did as a player.

And, oh yes, I met my future wife in Sweden in 1990. Sometimes I look at Camilla today, and our daughter, Elicia, and wonder what my life would have been like if I'd never returned to Sweden, if I had said no to managing the Bets.

I don't even want to think about it.

Chapter 29:

Success in Sweden

The Swedish Elite League is Sweden's major league. When I returned in 1990, the level of play was probably equal to the rookie leagues in America, and it was getting better every year. Also, the game was becoming more popular every year. There were eight teams in the Elite League that first year I managed in Rattvik, and by the mid-'90s that number had doubled.

Being an American didn't exactly make me a rarity. Quite a few teams had American managers, and almost every team had at least one coach who was a foreigner—American, Japanese, Cuban or whatever. Also, each club was allowed to carry as many foreign players as they wanted, although they could play only two at any one time so they usually signed only two. Foreigners usually made the most money, and they deserved it because with few exceptions they were the best ballplayers.

Helping to ease the transition for any American was the fact that most Swedish people under the age of forty, and some over it, spoke English. That was especially good for me, because I'm sorry to say I never did catch on to their language—either when I was there as a player or when I returned as a manager. If I listen to them talking I can get the gist of the conversation, but I could not join in.

The ballparks in Sweden have no lights because all through the season the sun never goes down. You can play catch at midnight, if you're so inclined. That's great if you love to play ball all day and all night, or if you're the one saving money on electricity at the ballpark. But it takes a little getting used to. I mean, it can really throw your body clock off quite drastically.

As when I was playing there, teams played two to four games a week, from April through August, with a three-week break in July for the national team tournament. Playoffs could last until late September.

The whole time I coached and managed in Sweden, I stayed busy when I got back to the States, too. I was operating the youth camps with Sal in Corning, helping to run the baseball camp in Ocala, and scouting. I had gotten into radio by then, too, and from 1992 to 2000 I did play-by-play on broadcasts of Elmira College men's hockey games, with Sal doing the color commentary. For some of that time I also announced on broadcasts of high school football and basketball games. In 2002-03, I was the color commentator with play-by-play man Tom Callahan for broadcasts of Elmira's minor-league hockey team, the Jackals.

When I went to Sweden I was still scouting for the White Sox after earlier stints as a scout for the Orioles and the Yankees. In 1992, I was hired as a scout by the expansion Florida Marlins, who were to start playing in the National League the following year. In 1996, I left the Marlins for the Atlanta Braves. Since the Marlins won their first World Series that year, it's a decision I'd like to forget, except that I went to work for Bill Clark, no relation, who was supervisor of scouting for the Braves and who became a good friend.

I had first met Bill when I was in Hunnewell and he was a scout for the Cincinnati Reds. During spring training in 1999, I was a coach for the Braves' International Coaches Clinic. But the Braves fired Bill and me after that season, and when he went to the San Diego Padres he took me along.

I'm pleased to say I played a role in helping some much younger players get their start in baseball, too. While I was in Sweden, I established the country's first Little League program. When play began in 1998, there were just two teams—one in Leksand and one in Rattvik—and in the very first game, on June 24, Leksand won 7–3.

I served as official scorekeeper for that game. A copy of the original scorecard is on display at the Little League Baseball Museum in Williamsport, Pennsylvania.

All the while, I was constantly reminded of the post-polio that had brought my playing days to an end. For the first time in my life, I found myself choosing activities based on whether I thought they would tax my limited energy supply. I'd always been willing and eager to try anything, and I probably did more things than many so-called able-bodied people—golfing, skiing, fishing, boating and bowling, for example.

I even scored a hole-in-one, a rarity for any golfer. It happened on August 6, 1991, at the Circle R Golf Course in Beaver Dams, New York, near Corning. I'd just had an awful time on the previous hole, shooting a ten or eleven, and I went up to the tee mad as hell and whacked the ball as hard as I could with my four-iron. The par-three hole was a hundred-and-forty-five-yard dogleg, and I hit the ball so far I couldn't follow its flight. Walking up the fairway with Camilla and my dad, who were playing with me, I searched everywhere but still couldn't find the ball.

"Where the hell is it?" I asked, really irritated now, as we neared the green.

"Beats me," said Dad, looking all around him.

Camilla went ahead of us. She walked onto the green and up to the cup. Then she bent down, reached into the hole and pulled out a ball. My ball.

It was the fourth hole, which made it even more special. Four has always been my favorite number, and I've worn it on my uniform whenever I've been able to get it—the number four itself or at least a number with the numeral four in it. The reason is that four was the great Lou Gehrig's number. I've never been a Yankee fan, but I've always felt a bond with Gehrig. Maybe it's because for a long time Lou Gehrig's disease—amyotrophic lateral sclerosis, or ALS—was believed to be a form of polio, and I still think of it that way. Gehrig had this disease at the end of his life, and I had polio at the beginning of mine. Gehrig pitched in college and played first base as a pro, and I also pitched and later played first base. Just some little things like that. I can't really explain it beyond that, but it's there, some kind of connection.

Anyway, my golfing days were behind me now. Most of my muscle loss had occurred in my arms, neck and upper back, and my arms tired very easily. At times, I even had trouble lifting them over my head. Playing darts one night, I felt the strain on my arm as I tried to get it in position to throw a dart. I found that if I overdid it physically, then I would get dizzy and woozy and also mentally fatigued. I tried to stay active, but I was learning to watch myself, pace myself, and monitor my activities.

For seven years, from 1994 through 1999 and again in 2002, I was the pitching coach for the Swedish Junior National Team. It's funny how I got the job. Mike Clancy, a transplanted American of twenty years, was hired as the manager, and he called one day and offered me a spot on his staff. I was hesitant at first because of what Mike and I had been through.

In 1990, when I was managing Rattvik, Mike was managing the Edsberg club and was also playing center field for them. We were battling them for the playoffs when the teams met late that season. In this particular game, Rattvik was batting in the bottom of the ninth, the score tied with runners at first and third and two outs.

I figured it was the perfect time for a trick play I'd had the team practicing all season. We worked on it for five minutes at every practice. It was a timing play that had to be executed to perfection, and this night we did it just as we'd practiced it.

Here's how it went: As the pitcher started into the stretch motion, the runner at first broke toward second in a sprint. Three things could happen at this point: The pitcher could stop his motion, which would be a balk and would move each runner up one base; the pitcher could come to the set position, then try to throw out the runner who was on the move; or they could just allow the runner to have second base. The first option would give us the winning run; the second could lead to us scoring the winning run; the third would just move up the runner from first, and we didn't want to settle for that.

The pitcher came set, then stepped off the rubber. As we'd practiced, the runner froze between first and second. I was coaching at third, and as the pitcher moved toward the runner and then started his throwing motion toward the shortstop covering second base, I sent the man at third toward the plate. He scored, and we won.

All of our players started piling on each other in celebration, and as I glanced at the scene I saw out of the corner of my eye that Clancy was charging in from center and heading straight for the runner who had broken from first and started it all. Clancy hit him with a forearm to the back of the neck, knocked him down and jumped on him, fists flying.

I hustled over and fell on top of Clancy and pounded him with my fists as he pounded my runner. Pretty soon other players came over and either pulled us off the pile or added to the beating. It was quite a scene.

All of that was still fresh in my mind when Mike called after getting the Junior National job.

"Well, I don't know, Mike," I said. "Do you think we could work together?"

"That's all in the past, Dave," he said. "I can forget it if you can. I'm just looking for the best pitching coach I can find to help these kids, and that's you. The job's yours if you'll take it."

I took it.

My last year with the Junior National team, 2002, was particularly special because the European Junior Championships were played in Sweden that year for the first time.

It was a thrill to be associated with the host team and country, but the experience was a bit frustrating because of the weather. Temperatures stayed in the fifties and sixties most of that summer, and it rained nearly every day.

We played a six-game exhibition tour in London and won two of those games. The wins weren't that important, though, because it was like spring training—the idea was to get the roster set, find out who you could count on and who you couldn't.

The sportswriters had picked us to finish sixth or seventh in the eight-team field, and after the first game it looked like they might be right. We got pummeled 11–2 by Slovakia.

The next day, we were down 6–3 to Romania with two outs in the ninth inning and nobody on, but we rallied to tie it and then won it in the thirteenth inning. That turned it around for us, and we didn't lose again until we met England on the final day, with an outside chance for the gold medal. We had to beat England and get some help in other games, but we lost 5–3 and finished second, taking the silver medal. It was Sweden's highest finish ever in the European Championships, and we were thrilled.

The European Championships was one of two tournaments the junior team played in each year. The other was the Nordic Championships, with Sweden joined by Finland, Denmark and Norway. Sweden always won the gold at the Nordic event, but the European was another story. Taking second place there was something special.

I was with Rattvik for three years in the Nineties—as manager in 1990 and as pitching coach in 1993 and '94. Frankly, it was a lousy club when I got there—a last-place team that was the laughingstock of the league. The year before I arrived, they had won only three of forty-two games.

We lost our first four games that first season, and the media—no less critical than their toughest American counterparts, and worse than most—started referring to the Bets as "Dave and the Mistakes." That was *their* mistake.

The Bets joined the playoff hunt and stayed there right up to the last weekend of the season. Going into the final two games, we needed only to split to make the playoffs for the first time since 1981. But that's a lot easier said than done.

We were on the road, playing the Kungsangen Kings, the team we were battling with for that final playoff spot. We lost big on Saturday, and that set up a showdown on Sunday, winner take all.

I gave the guys a fiery pre-game speech and they responded, building a 7–1 lead after five innings. But the Kings kept fighting back, getting it to 7–5, then 7–6 after eight. In the bottom of the ninth, with the score still 7–6, our closer, my old friend Magnus Hoglund, came in to finish it off. Magnus, a right-hander, had done it all as a pitcher—starter, long relief, middle relief, short relief—and he continued to do it long after this. When I spoke with him after the 2005 season, he had just retired as a player at the age of forty-four. He was still pitching during that final season, and effectively. I envy the guy.

In this game, he got the first two batters in the ninth, no problem, and we were one out away. But three straight singles tied the score and sent the game into extra innings, and now the Kings had momentum on their side.

After a scoreless tenth, we pushed across a run in the eleventh inning. But our closer was out of the game now, and we couldn't hold them. The Kings got a single and a two-run homer to win it and send us packing.

It was a somber group that made the four-hour bus ride back to Rattvik—one of the quietest trips I've ever been on. The next day we had an end-of-season meeting, and then everyone went their separate ways.

As I think about it now, it had been a pretty good season. We'd accomplished a lot more than probably any of us expected we would, and certainly more than the fans and the media expected.

Still, I've never really gotten over the way my first season as manager ended. It made it very difficult to walk away from that team, but a deal was a deal, and I had agreed to start up the baseball camp for disabled kids with Sal back home the next summer. So I packed up after that season and went back to Corning, not knowing what my future in Rattvik would be—or, in fact, if I had a future there at all.

I did, though. The two years that I came back as pitching coach, the Bets made it to the playoffs. The team had continued to improve, building on the foundation I had helped start there.

I've always felt proud of that.

Chapter 30:

The Ugly American

Late in the 1993 season, I had a run-in with a player on the Rattvik Bets.

Actually, he was a player/coach named Steve. His last name escapes me and, really, it isn't important now. What happened is significant, though, because it's the only time I ever had a serious incident involving a player on my team while I was a manager or coach—and only the second time ever that I had a fight with a player on my team, the one with the left-fielder in Beeville being the first.

I was the Bets' pitching coach. Steve was an American who had pitched in college, played some Double-A ball in the States and was now the Rattvik shortstop.

Steve disliked me right from the start. Maybe, because he had once been a pitcher, he thought he should have been the pitching coach instead of me. We never discussed it, though, so that's just a guess.

In general, Steve went around with a chip on his shoulder, playing the Ugly American for all it was worth. A lot of the players and even the manager were intimidated by him, but I wasn't.

This one game, with an opposing runner on second base and less than two outs, Steve went deep into the hole at short for a grounder and backhanded the ball as the runner broke for third. For some reason I'll never understand, Steve didn't throw the ball but instead just stuck it in his glove and started walking toward third. By the time he got there, the runner was already on the bag and was standing there talking to the third-base coach.

Steve walked up behind the runner and gave him a two-handed chop to the neck, and the runner went down hard. The guy got up and whacked Steve with his helmet, and now we had a real brawl.

I went out from the dugout and grabbed our pitcher. I did that for two reasons. One, I didn't want him getting involved and maybe getting hurt. And two, I wasn't going in there to defend Steve.

Not only did Steve never treat me with any respect or even decency, but he'd just done something so stupid I figured he deserved whatever beating he got. I'd have been right in the middle of it if it had been any of our other guys, but as far as I was concerned, Steve was on his own.

Well, he survived. In fact, somehow he came away looking like a victim, and acting pretty smug for having managed it. The runner was ejected, apparently because the umpires had failed to see what Steve did and only saw the runner come back at him. Besides that, the runner was called out, don't ask me why or how.

None of it made any sense.

Steve came into the dugout gloating. I went up to him and got in his face.

"Wipe that smirk off!" I yelled. "What you just did out there was the most bush-league play I've ever seen. You're the one who should have been thrown out, and you know it."

He yelled back at me, and we went on that way for a while, until a few players got between us and moved us apart.

When that half-inning was over, our team took the field again. I was still so mad I couldn't sit, so I walked up and down the dugout while our guys took infield.

Suddenly, out of the corner of my eye I saw a movement, and instinctively I lifted the clipboard I was carrying in one hand and got it up to my face just as a baseball came smashing into it. The ball and the clipboard rattled around the dugout while I tried to figure out what had just happened.

I looked out toward shortstop and saw Steve with that smirk on his face again. He'd purposely thrown wild to first base—and I mean wild, since the bag was well up the line from our dugout—and tried to bean me. He'd nearly succeeded, too. If I hadn't gotten that clipboard up just in time, the ball probably would have done considerable damage to my head.

I stood frozen and seethed for a while, then finally sat and seethed some more and waited out that half inning. It seemed to last forever.

When the side was retired and our guys came into the dugout again, I was waiting for Steve and he knew it. He came right at me and I moved toward him. He threw a punch and I threw one, and we wrestled each other to the floor of the dugout.

Both of us got hurt, but not badly, before the other players pulled us apart.

"If I was the manager, you'd be gone," I yelled at Steve.

But I wasn't the manager, and the manager wasn't about to do anything about what had just happened. The league did something, though—not because of the fight, but because of the incident at third base. Officials looked at the tape of the game, saw what had happened and suspended Steve for several games.

The Bets got hot after that. We won the final twelve games of the season and qualified for the playoffs.

Just before our first playoff game, Steve asked to talk to me.

"Look," he said, "I'm sorry for the way I treated you. I never gave you a chance. I just decided you weren't the guy for the job. I was pretty rough on you."

I didn't let him get off that easy.

"It's a little late for that," I said. "What you've done has disrupted the whole team. You've made my job a lot harder. The season's almost over now. This won't help any of us, except maybe you. Maybe it'll help you feel better about yourself.

"I'll accept your apology," I said, "but I won't forget what you've done."

And I never did.

I got fired after the 1994 season. I call it being fired, anyway, but technically what happened is that Rattvik and I had reached a verbal agreement right after the season that I would return for two more years as manager, then I got a call in November informing me that the board of directors had decided not to bring me back.

They said they had decided they couldn't afford me, but I think they just were ready to get rid of me for some reason. The salary we'd agreed to hadn't changed in the month and a half or so since I'd left Sweden, so that wasn't it.

In any case, I was gone. My firing came as quite a shock, especially after I'd begun a rebuilding program that, incidentally, was to keep the Bets strong throughout that decade.

Now I had no job. Worse, I had met the woman I intended to marry during the 1990 season, and Camilla Ahnstrom and I were living together. I had to find some way to get back to Sweden.

Maybe because of what I had been through before—the injury that ended my pitching career and the post-polio syndrome that ended my playing career—I didn't see this as something that would stop me. I remember thinking that I would just catch on somewhere. That had become the pattern for my life: One door closes and another one opens.

I felt confident that it would happen again. And it did.

CHAPTER 31:

FINDING LOVE

In 1990, I shared an apartment in Rattvik with our only "foreign import player," as they were called. He was a fellow American named Tom Nolan, a pitcher from Chicago.

I brought Tom to Sweden to pitch for the Bets. A onetime draft pick of the San Diego Padres, he had pitched for the Indianapolis Clowns in the mid-'80s, when I was a co-owner of the team and its manager and first baseman.

Tom was getting up in age for a baseball player by the time he got to Sweden, but he could still pitch, and Rattvik needed an import pitcher. It seemed like a good arrangement for both sides. But despite Tom's best efforts, both he and the team got off to a rough start.

What complicated matters even more was the fact that I had to play Tom out of position, and use him as a pitcher. Tom was becoming increasingly frustrated on the field and I couldn't blame him.

Tom was doing just fine off the field, though, and so was I. He was dating three or four women at once, and I had four or five regular dates. I guess that didn't satisfy either of us, though, because we were always looking for other women. And we didn't have much trouble finding them.

It's funny about me and women. Some of them automatically ruled me out as a potential partner because of what they saw as my physical limitations. Others found me irresistible, and there were many of those.

As for me, when I was young I thought of chasing after women as just another game. I took pride in getting a lot of women, scoring as often as I could. The more I got, the more I felt like a man. It somehow proved my "normalcy"—or so I thought. If I could beat another guy to a woman or score with more women than he did, that showed—in my mind, at that time—that despite my limitations I was a better man than he was. And I thought other guys would look up to me because of it.

In 1984, I met a beautiful blonde in Florida while I was working with a physical therapist to rehab my elbow. I was part-owner of the Indianapolis Clowns at the time, and was operating the baseball camp in Ocala, and Dawn was an intern at the physical therapist's office.

We dated for months, and things were definitely starting to heat up. I wouldn't say I was in love with her, but I felt I was headed in that direction.

Dawn would occasionally follow the Clowns on the road, meeting me at various stops along the way and staying with me for a few days here and there. After that season, she even came to Corning and spent about a week with me, getting to know my hometown and my family and friends.

She was an outdoors type who liked to jog, bike and hike in the woods—that kind of thing. At some point, I guess she realized that I'd never share her interest in those activities, and that we'd never be able to go jogging or biking or hiking together. So one day—this was after I had my surgery and had gone to Tampa with Dad to visit my brother Dan, who lived there—she just sat me down and told me straight out that it was over. She said she didn't see a future for us, and so she didn't want to spend time with me anymore.

I respected her for being honest with me about how she felt, but still it hurt. For a while it hurt a lot, and then I took the attitude that, well, if that's the way she wanted it, that was fine with me. It was her loss, not mine. I came to grips with it and was able to move on with my life.

Some women found it absolutely amazing that I could do the things I did with my physical limitations. And I suppose there were others who didn't focus much on my limitations, maybe didn't pay much attention to the crutches or the leg brace, and just accepted me as another guy.

Whatever the case, there were enough women in my life that I never felt at a disadvantage to anybody. The only time I doubted that I'd ever find one I could love, and who would love me back, was during that dark period right after my playing career ended.

But I wasn't even looking for love during those days in Sweden. And, as things sometimes happen, that's when and where I found it.

On April 19, 1990, Tom Nolan and I went to a rock concert after practice. The concert was at Rattvik's Folkparken and featured the Swedish rock band Shaboom.

We didn't go for the music. Heck, we didn't even actually go into the park. We just hung around outside the gates, waiting for the concert to end so we could round up the females as they came out.

Speaking English was a chick magnet, and we had several girls engaged in a lively conversation with us as the park emptied. I noticed at one point that Tom had drifted over to this gorgeous blonde who walked by a few yards beyond our group. He got to talking to her as she stopped under a street lamp, and their conversation went on for quite a while.

Finally, I excused myself and left the group of girls I was talking with and went over and joined Tom and his blonde. Tom introduced us, just being polite, but I could tell he wanted to get back to his private conversation with this girl he called Camilla.

I broke away, walked down the block and waited under another street lamp. All the while, I couldn't take my eyes off this girl. I kept wishing it was me she was talking to, and not Tom.

Camilla remembers: "I was waiting for my ride outside the concert, and this man came up to me and started speaking English. I talked to him for a few minutes, and he seemed nice, and I thought this was so cool. I wasn't used to speaking English.

"I remember Dave leaning against a light pole, chewing gum and trying to look cool or something. Looking back, I don't even think I remember seeing any crutches or anything that made him look different."

Eventually, the happy couple broke it up, and Tom came walking my way, a big smile on his face.

"So?" I said.

"So I got her phone number," he said.

All the way home, I had to listen to him talk about her. It was Camilla this, and Camilla that. And there was more when we got back to the apartment.

Over the next several days, Tom called her number I don't know how many times. But Camilla never went out with him. Tom let it drop eventually, and we went on with the baseball season, which was turning out to be a lot better than anyone had expected, with Rattvik in the thick of the playoff race.

Tom was the only import player on the roster. Each team was allowed to play two foreigners, and every other team was at the limit, but we had only Tom, and he gave it his best shot, but he couldn't lift the team himself.

At the apartment we shared, Tom's bedroom was right down the hall from mine. One night he brought a brunette home with him. He'd told me earlier that this girl claimed to be a witch and that they were going to have a séance that night. I didn't want anything to do with that stuff, so not long after they came in I headed off to my room to read for a while and then go to sleep.

As I was lying in bed, I could smell incense or something burning, and I could hear chanting coming from the direction of Tom's bedroom. I tried to laugh it off, but it was kind of eerie. After a while, I was getting drowsy and was just about to put the book down and turn off the light, when I heard the chanting grow louder and louder. Then suddenly all the lights in the apartment went out.

Now I was wide awake again.

I lay there in the dark for a long time, waiting for someone to come into my room, but no one did. Eventually, I drifted off to sleep, but I was jolted awake when the light beside my bed suddenly came on. After a while, I heard the "witch" leave and I turned over and dropped off again, this time into a deep sleep.

The next morning I told Tom I never wanted that woman in the apartment again. And I never did see her after that. In fact, pretty soon Tom was gone too.

In mid-July we had a team appearance at a swanky downtown restaurant, and Tom got a little drunk and called the board president's wife a bitch to her face. Never mind that she *was* one; he probably shouldn't have told her so. A few days later, Tom had a plane ticket back to Chicago.

He left a few things behind, including a scrap of paper with a phone number and Camilla Ahnstrom's name scrawled on it. I found it one day when I was cleaning up.

It took a little while, but finally I got up the nerve to call the number. A young girl answered, speaking Swedish. She couldn't speak any English, and I had an awful time trying to get her to understand that I wanted to speak to Camilla. (Later, I learned this was Camilla's five-year-old sister, Bea.)

Finally, the girl put the phone down, and there was a long silence. I didn't know whether to hang on or hang up. I waited, and soon another, older, voice came on, also speaking Swedish.

I answered her in English, and when she realized I couldn't speak Swedish she talked to me in English, with a thick accent.

Camilla said she remembered me, but I'm not sure she really did. We talked for a while and agreed to meet in Falun, where she lived. We set the date for July 25, the next day the Bets had off. I was to meet Camilla at the first bus stop that I came to in Falun as I drove from Rattvik.

That day, I made the hour's drive to Falun and nearly missed the connection. I drove right past the first bus stop, but I caught a glimpse of a blonde standing on the corner, and I turned around about a mile down the road. When I came back, there she was.

Camilla recalls: "I vaguely remembered Dave from meeting him a few months back. I was very excited to talk to him, and we hit it off right away. My English wasn't that good, but we managed to keep a conversation going. He was a really nice guy, and different in a good way. I don't think his disability had any impact on me in a negative way.

"He was always a gentleman. He was a very caring person. He would open the door for me, he would buy presents for me, and I wasn't used to that at such a young age, only sixteen."

We spent the whole day and evening together. We ate, played miniature golf, sat on the beach at the lake, went for a drive, and ate again. When I dropped her off at the apartment where she lived with her mother and two sisters, it was about ten at night.

Then I made the hour-long drive back to Rattvik, with Camilla on my mind the whole time.

Pretty soon Camilla was the only woman in my life. We began seeing each other often. If I couldn't get to Falun, she would take the bus to Rattvik and spend a few days there before returning home when the team went on the road.

One Sunday afternoon as I sat on the hood of my car waiting for her, I was shocked to see an old girlfriend of mine get off the bus just ahead of Camilla. Maria came walking in my direction, with Camilla trailing right behind, when suddenly Maria spotted me and shrieked, "Hi, Dave!" and came over to the car. Camilla came with her, a cold expression on her beautiful face, her eyes firing invisible darts.

I had no choice but to introduce them. It was a little awkward for a few minutes there. Then Maria clumsily said goodbye, Camilla climbed in the car and we drove to my place in silence. Camilla wouldn't talk to me.

It was our first disagreement of any kind. But we survived it.

Our relationship continued to strengthen and deepen, and after that season Camilla decided she wanted to come to the States with me. This was a big decision for her, because she had never been far from home before.

Right after the season, Camilla and I traveled by car and boat to London, where we were to meet my mom and dad for a Eurail train trip that would take us to Spain, France, Italy and Germany. (In Germany, I would take a chisel and hammer and cut myself a piece of the Berlin Wall, which they were tearing down at the time.)

We met up in London on September 6, my thirty-eighth birthday. It was good to see my parents again, and great to be able to introduce them to Camilla.

After we picked up my parents at the airport, and we all settled into our hotel, we slept most of the day. I remember looking at Mom, Dad and Camilla as they slept and getting that feeling you get as a kid when you know you're safe and secure. It had been a long time since I'd felt that way.

When we got back from the trip, we all spent a couple of days in Rattvik and then drove to Falun to have dinner at Camilla's place. Camilla's parents had been divorced for less than a year, so it was just her mom and two sisters—Kim, who is a year younger than Camilla, and Beatrice, who is ten years younger. (Later, when Camilla's mother married Per Johansson, that union produced a half-sister, Nathalie.)

It was a sad scene when we had to leave for Stockholm and the flight to the U.S. Watching Camilla and her mom saying goodbye was tough. I could see that they loved each other very much.

"It was very, very difficult—the hardest thing that I've ever done in my life," Camilla remembers. "I was only sixteen years old, I didn't drive, my English wasn't that good, and I had no family or friends in the States. It was very hard, and I'm not sure I would do it again."

It takes a very brave woman to do what Camilla was doing. I admired her for it, and still do.

CHAPTER 32:

TYING THE KNOT

Camilla was very lonely at first. She missed her family and she missed her homeland, and I had some idea of how she felt. It was similar for me when I first went to Sweden. And, in fact, I felt the same kind of loneliness whenever Camilla returned home for a visit.

She stayed with me in Corning on a three-month tourist visa. Over the next few years, she'd go home and then come back again, then go home again, then come back. Eventually, the separations grew shorter and fewer, until finally we no longer traveled alone and no longer were apart.

I was coaching or managing in the Swedish Elite League through 1998, and I also was coaching Sweden's Junior National Team. Each time I came back home, Camilla came with me. If Camilla traveled back to Sweden for the holidays, I went with her.

This led to extended stays for Camilla in Corning. And this meant that she was here illegally on a regular basis. Still on a three-month visa for each visit, she would stay five or six months at a time.

In November of 1995, as we came into the U.S. from Sweden, Camilla was pulled aside by Immigration officials at Baltimore-Washington International Airport. They took her into an interrogation room off to the side and wouldn't let me in there with her. Three hours later, after much heated discussion and threats to send her back to Sweden that night, Camilla was granted a one-time humanitarian visa.

That allowed her to stay with me for ninety days, but for the last time. She would not be allowed in the country on a temporary visa again. And if she overstayed her ninety days, we were assured that people would be sent to get her and deport her. This really put a scare into us.

What they were saying, in other words—and they came right out and said it, in fact—was that Camilla would not be allowed in the United States again if we didn't get married. If we did get married, she'd be eligible for full citizenship.

Talk about putting pressure on a guy! Well, Camilla and I had discussed marriage anyway. We just didn't know when or where it would happen. I couldn't talk her into getting married at home plate, the way Don Zimmer had done with his bride at Dunn Field back in Elmira, so the wedding had to be scheduled in baseball's off-season.

We set the date for November 28, 1995. We were married at the Erwin Town Hall in Painted Post, by the Justice of the Peace. Jeff Moshier, a good family friend, was my best man. My parents were the only other people there.

Following a wedding dinner at the Olive Garden restaurant near Arnot Mall in Big Flats, Camilla and I got away for a quick three-day honeymoon in Syracuse. While we were there, I couldn't resist: The Syracuse Crunch were home, so I took her to an American Hockey League game.

How Camilla has put up with me and our lifestyle, I'll never know. It sure hasn't been easy. I believe it takes a very special, very supportive person to be part of the life of a professional athlete, manager or coach. During the season, there are many separations, and very little quality time for partners or family members. Both parties in a marriage have to be very trusting of each other. And we were.

Camilla has always supported me and often has given up what she wanted in order to allow me to do my job and chase my dream. She is a beautiful person inside as well as out. I'm so lucky to have found her.

On August 15, 1999, two weeks ahead of schedule, we became three.

Camilla delivered a beautiful, healthy little baby girl whom we named Eva Lillian Elicia Clark—or Little Boogerhead for short. Elicia, as we call her now, was born at the hospital in Falun, Sweden, while I was in the country as a roving scout and instructor for Major League Baseball International.

I was working with a team just an hour's drive from Falun that day and was able to make it home for the birth of Elicia. I even got to cut the umbilical cord. Our daughter's birth was a very special moment, and I'm so glad I was able to be there for it.

"We were both very happy when she was born," Camilla recalls. "Dave has always been a great dad from day one. There are some things that he just wasn't able to do, as far as pushing a stroller or carrying her around. But he made up for it in other ways, always showing her a lot of love."

Now I was just beginning a whole new part of my life. I began to realize how my parents must have felt when I came into the world—their first-born. I had feelings I'd never felt before, responsibilities I'd never had to deal with, hopes and fears and dreams I'd never experienced.

Now I was a daddy.

CHAPTER 33:

STORYBOOK YEAR

The Swedish Elite team in Leksand was looking for a pitching coach during the off-season of 1994–95, after I was fired by Rattvik.

They had just fired a guy named Glen Godwin, who was a very good friend of mine, and the thought of going after his job—even if it wasn't really his anymore—made me a little uncomfortable. But Leksand is located just about twenty miles down the road from Rattvik. If I could get that job, I thought, Camilla and I wouldn't even have to move. Besides, Leksand and Rattvik are arch-rivals, and if I was going to stay in baseball in Sweden, then why not move to the other side of that rivalry? I thought it might be fun.

I sent in my application, and they offered me the job. They were paying a lot less money than I had been making at Rattvik, though, and Camilla and I had long talks about it. Wasn't I worth more? Could we live on what they were offering? But wasn't this what I wanted to do? And couldn't it lead to something better? Finally, we decided I should take it, and I did.

Now I was forty-two years old and making another fresh start.

I spent the next four seasons with the Leksand Lumberjacks—two as pitching coach, then two as manager. Unlike Rattvik, Leksand was a team with a winning tradition, and fans and the media had high expectations year after year. I'm proud to say that tradition continued all four years I was with the Lumberjacks.

In 1995, we tied Skelleftea for first place in the league but lost out to them on the tiebreaker. We made it through two rounds of the playoffs, though, and met Skelleftea in what I think of as the Swedish World Series. That was a thrill—my first time in the finals.

Skelleftea is an eleven-hour bus ride north of Leksand. It is just south of the Arctic Circle, so it can be, and usually is, extremely cold by late September when the championship round is played. This year, it was.

We won the first game 5–3, scoring two runs in the eighth inning. Then we lost three in a row to put ourselves in a deep hole in the best-of-seven series, especially with the games going back to their place. Magnus Hoglund pitched a gem for us in Game Five and we won 3–0. Now we were back in it.

The next day, the umpire missed the call on a crucial play at second base in the bottom of the fourth, costing us a double play and leading to an early exit for me. We were down 1–0 at the time and Skelleftea had the bases loaded with one out. A double play would have gotten us out of it, and we'd have had some momentum on our side. But the ump ruled our shortstop didn't touch the bag at second, and so a second run scored and they still had runners at second and third, now with two outs.

I came out and yelled and carried on and, frankly, went a little nuts. The umpire ejected me and started walking away, and I grabbed his shoulder and spun him around. That's a no-no in any country, and naturally I knew it. But I kept it up, and it was a good ten minutes before they got me off the field and out of the dugout.

After order was finally restored, Skelleftea scored four more runs that inning to go up 6–0 heading to the fifth. They went on to beat us that night, and the series was over, four games to two.

The media had a field day with the whole incident at second base. My picture was all over the papers, and every TV station played tape of my ranting, over and over again. They also showed clips that proved the shortstop had stepped on the bag just as I'd claimed he did.

Camilla read all of it, and watched it on TV, and told me, "Sometimes you embarrass me."

An old friend of the family who lives in Skelleftea sent my mother-in-law a lengthy newspaper article with a huge color photo of me being tossed and wrote to her, "Is this your son-in-law?"

League officials took notice, too. They fined me and gave me a two-game suspension, to be served at the start of the next season.

I'll admit my temper got the best of me. Despite my best efforts to keep it under control, I still explode from time to time. It's just that burning desire to win, to succeed, that makes me act that way.

Despite all the trouble over that double play, it was such a great experience to be in the championship finals. It had now been eight years since Leksand had last won the championship—a long drought for that franchise—and I came out of that season determined to help the team take that last big step again.

In 1996, I was signed again as the pitching coach. My contract had a clause that would let me go to Atlanta, Georgia, for the Summer Olympics if I got the opportunity, which I intended to pursue. As it turns out, I was selected as the baseball supervisor of sports information for Team USA. My job was to make sure results, rosters and statistics were distributed to the media and the teams, and also to see that umpires got to their games on time and that game balls were ready for play.

Team USA finished third that year, taking the bronze medal. It was an honor to have been associated with that team and the Olympic Games.

After the Games, it was back to Sweden. It had been quite a whirlwind trip. From home in Falun to Atlanta, here's how it went: drive a hundred and fifty miles to Stockholm; fly to London, then to Washington, then to the Elmira-Corning Regional Airport; then drive to Atlanta, picking up Camilla on the way (she had flown into Baltimore). It was pretty much the same thing in reverse when it was all over. Still, because of the Swedish Elite League's three-week summer break, I missed only four of Leksand's games.

The Lumberjacks won the regular-season championship, swept the first two rounds of playoffs and then, as fate would have it, met my old Rattvik club in the finals. It was their first trip ever to the title round, and we continued our sweep, knocking the Bets out in four games. Now we were the champions.

To cap off a storybook year, that November I attended a dinner in Boston where I received the national Giant Steps Coaching Award, a great honor. Dick Schaap, who was a terrific writer and sportscaster, was master of ceremonies for the program, and I was thrilled to meet him. Richard Lapchick, who is well known and highly regarded in and out of the world of sports, presented me with the award, and I was as proud as could be to accept it from him.

Richard is the one who nominated me, and I will forever be grateful for that. Richard, son of the late and great basketball coach Joe Lapchick, had polio himself as a young boy, so he had some empathy for my situation. After learning something about my life and my career in sports, he made the nomination. We've kept in touch ever since, and I'm proud to say I consider him a friend. As I write this, Richard is director of the DeVos Sport Business Management Program at the University of Central Florida.

The winners of the Giant Steps Awards, which are presented annually by the Northeastern University Center for the Study of Sport and Society and the National Consortium for Academics and Sports, were announced earlier that year, 1996. I was invited to Washington, D.C., to receive the personal congratulations of President Bill Clinton and Hillary Clinton, and to get a tour of the White House.

In each case—at the White House and at the awards ceremony in Boston—I felt a little out of my element. Quite a lot, actually. But in each case, the reception I received from the moment I arrived made my apprehension melt away. In Washington, President Clinton embraced me. In Boston, at the reception before the banquet, people came up to me in a steady stream, thanking me for having inspired them.

I can't really describe how proud or how grateful I felt.

In 1997, I was named manager of the Leksand Lumberjacks. I didn't really want the job, because it took me away from working with the pitchers, which I really enjoyed and got a lot of satisfaction from. Besides, when you're coming off a championship season there's only one way you can go, unless you repeat as champs—and that's down. From the start, the media and the fans made it clear to me that anything short of another title would be deemed a failure. I took the job anyway.

There was some question as to whether I could go from being pitching coach to manager, even though I'd already managed successfully at Rattvik. I felt as though I was under a magnifying glass. Every move I made was questioned by fans and reporters. Fortunately, we got off to a good start, winning eight of our first nine games.

Little did I know that I'd get to work with the pitchers even in my new position as manager. My pitching coach was fired, against my wishes, midway through the season and was not replaced.

That season, I had the pleasure of leading the Lumberjacks to victory over the Bets, on national TV, in the first game ever played at Rattvik's new stadium. In the ninth inning, I got into an argument with an umpire and probably came close to being ejected. Camilla, who was at the game, told me later the crowd was chanting for me to get tossed, which surprised me because I really didn't hear them. And as before, she told me how much this embarrassed her.

Camilla says: "Dave hates to lose. Sometimes he would make it clear during a game that he wasn't happy, and a couple of times he got thrown out. One time he just sat down on home plate. I would hear people talking about him, and I felt like hiding under my seat. It was very embarrassing. I'm glad I didn't see more than a couple of those things happen."

I guess I did all right as manager. We won the regular season title again and went into the postseason on a roll.

In the playoff opener, I pulled my starting pitcher, who was the ace of the staff, after he threw a fit when I went out to talk to him. The stadium was packed, and there we were, shouting at each other on the mound. I had no choice but to send him to the showers. And I had to bring in a reliever who really didn't have enough time to warm up. Fortunately, we were able to pull out a win. I hate to think how I would have been second-guessed if we'd lost that game.

We made it to the finals again, against our old nemesis, Skelleftea. Leksand had last beaten them in the finals in 1988.

The final round was a week late getting started because we hit a bad stretch of cold and rainy weather. It must have been bad if we didn't play, because not much stopped the games in Sweden. We even made a trip to Skelleftea and sat around in our hotel rooms for four days before we finally gave up and returned to Leksand. The league had to rework the whole schedule.

We won the series four games to one, clinching the title at home. Camilla was there, and she came down out of the stands and onto the field to celebrate with me to the playing of "We Are the Champions" by Queen over the public address system.

Mom and Dad were supposed to come over for the series, but Mom was in Corning Hospital being treated for shingles, and Dad of course stayed home to be with her. I called them from the clubhouse after we clinched, and told them how much I wished they could have been there. They were as happy for me as I was for myself and for our team.

As I soaked in all the excitement of the championship, I thought of my parents and all they had done for me and all they meant to me. I knew I wouldn't have been there without them. While I had them on the phone, I told them so.

CHAPTER 34:

GOODBYE, MOM

Mom died on November 26, 1997, the day before Thanksgiving. I was with her in her room at St. Joseph's Hospital in Elmira when she passed away. I remember looking at the clock when I knew she was gone. It was three-fifteen in the morning.

Mom was sixty-nine years old—too young, much too young. Her death left me devastated and thrust me into one of the darkest periods of my life.

I knew Mom hadn't been well, and that's why she and Dad had to pass up the chance to see us win the championship that year in Leksand. But as it turned out, we were told that the shingles that had put her in Corning Hospital at that time was just a minor complication related somehow to what was really ailing her—cancer of the lymph nodes. None of us, including Dad, had any idea how sick Mom was until just weeks before she died.

Looking back later, I realized Mom didn't seem her old self when she and Dad picked us up at the airport in Baltimore when Camilla and I flew home on October 13. But it didn't register that something very serious might be wrong with her.

On the drive home from the airport that time, we stopped for lunch at a Cracker Barrel restaurant in York, Pennsylvania. Camilla took a picture of Mom and me sitting out front in white wooden rockers. It's the last picture ever taken of us together, and I treasure it.

A few weeks after I got home, Mom and I had appointments with the same doctor, Michael Cilip, on the same afternoon. She was going to have him check out her back, which had been giving her problems ever since I'd returned from Sweden. I needed to have him remove a couple of worts.

Mom went in to see the doc first and then left, since we'd driven in separate cars. As Doctor Cilip and I were talking, he said something to me about Mom's condition, using the word "cancer" for the first time, and it nearly floored me. I had no idea she had cancer. The shock I felt must have shown on my face, because Doctor Cilip quickly apologized for letting it slip like that. Obviously, he thought we all knew, but Mom hadn't said a word.

When I left the doctor's office, I was a mess. Too many emotions were crowding my brain. I was hurt, scared, angry, you name it. The one I was angry at was Dad, for not telling me, so I went looking for him to give him a piece of my mind. Corning isn't that big a town, and as it happened, we passed each other driving in opposite directions on Pulteney Street, one of the main thoroughfares. I signaled Dad to pull over and then barked at him to follow me to the apartment where he and Mom were living on Fuller Avenue while their new house on Winfield Street was being finished.

When we pulled into the driveway, I hopped out of my car and hustled over to his pickup truck and demanded, "Why didn't you tell me?"

"Tell you what?" he said, and I knew from the puzzled expression on his face that he had no idea what I was talking about. He hadn't known, either.

When I told him, we both just collapsed onto the steps of the back porch and started crying uncontrollably. We must have been a pitiful sight, but we both hurt so bad, we didn't care if anybody saw us or, if they did, what they thought. It was a dark, dark day for us, and one that I would never want to relive.

Through all her doctor's appointments, all her treatments, Mom had never let on how serious her condition was. But that was Mom. She kept her problems to herself and dealt with them in her own way.

When I look back on my life, I feel as though a lot of her has rubbed off on me.

In this case, I think Mom honestly felt she was going to beat the cancer, and then she'd tell us all about it later. She'd had cancer once before, in fact—ovarian cancer, in the 1960s—and had survived it, at a time when the cancer survival rates were a lot lower.

I was only ten or so at that time, and I had no idea what was happening, so the details really didn't stay with me. I do remember that Mom had surgery and was in the hospital for a while, and that Grandma Z came to live with us and care for us while she was away. But I don't recall how long a period that was, or just when Mom came back home.

What I do remember, and vividly, is walking out to our big front porch one evening and finding Dad standing there in the dark, weeping. When he realized I was there he tried to hide the fact that he'd been crying, but it was too late.

"What's wrong, Dad?" I asked.

"I miss your Mom," he said, sniffling and reaching for his handkerchief. "I wish we could bring her home, now."

"I miss her too," I said.

And I did miss her, very much. Mom and I had always been as close as a parent and child could be. It's been the same for me with Dad.

Many kids, if not most, seem to be embarrassed easily and frequently by things their parents say or do. I've never felt that way. I've always been happy to have my parents around, and as proud of them as they've been of me.

When I was going to school, Mom used to drive me right to the door every day, and she'd be there to pick me up later. This started in elementary school and continued right through high school. Most kids probably would have rather walked or taken the bus, but not me. I was never embarrassed to have my mom drive me.

After third grade, I transferred from Corning's Hugh Gregg Elementary School to Kent Phillips Elementary School, because from the Gregg school you had to go to another school for grades four through six, and that place had a lot of steps. So I went to Kent Phillips for those three grades, and then I moved on to what was Northside Blodgett Junior High School.

Northside Blodgett has steps, too, and now there was no getting around them. Or so it seemed. But Mom made special arrangements for me, and every day she would drive me to a particular entrance where the principal, whose name was Gerald Vine, would meet us and carry me up a flight of steps to the first floor.

As little kids playing ball, we always want to have our parents at the games. But after a while we can be embarrassed just to have them show up, and it's definitely not cool if they come up to you after a game and give you a big hug for something you did, or just because your team won. But I was always proud to have my parents anywhere with me, and eager to show them how I felt and to have them show me how they felt.

There's a photo that was taken outside the stadium in Jacksonville, Florida, after a game I played with the Indianapolis Clowns. I'm all sweaty in my uniform, but the three of us—Mom, Dad and me—are warmly embracing, and you can just see that we are all proud and happy to be there. It's one of my favorite pictures.

Eventually, Mom did come home from the hospital during that first bout with cancer. But it was a long time before I was able to appreciate what she'd been through and what a miracle it was that she was able to survive it. It gave me a better understanding of just where I get all my spunk and determination. Neither of my parents had a "give-up" bone in their body.

When Mom died, I took on all the responsibilities. I handled the funeral arrangements, the notices, the calls to family and friends, the straightening out of my parents' personal papers and effects, talking with the preacher and to lawyers and insurance agents about estate laws and transfers, and all the other details that follow a death and which you attend to in a state of numbness.

Something inside me died when Mom passed away. I lost a little of that security feeling you have as a member of a family. I lost a little innocence along with it. In some ways, I would never be the same.

During my baseball career and travels, I'd said goodbye to my parents many times. It never got easier, as you might think it would. There were always plenty of tears shed as I got ready to leave.

The morning of Mom's funeral, I sat at the kitchen table in our apartment and wrote her a long letter. In it, I told her how badly I wished that our goodbye that day could be like all the others, when we knew that at the end of the journey we would see each other again. I told her how much she meant to me, and tried to express how much I would miss her—though words, even now, can't do it nearly well enough.

When it was time to say my final goodbye, I tucked the letter into the casket, kissed Mom softly, and took one long last look at her through the tears that welled up in my eyes. At the cemetery, I kissed her casket before they lowered it into the ground on a rather warm day for November 29. And then she was gone.

But in a way, Mom is still with me, a part of everything I do and everything I am. I'm always aware that nothing I've accomplished could have been done without the greatest parents anybody's ever had. They've been more than parents; they've been my heroes and my best and closest friends.

In my memory, Mom will always be a lively, hard-working, vibrant and beautiful person. She was a devoted wife and mother, a great cook and a tremendous business person. She was tough, but she was fair.

Mom had a very strong work ethic, and she passed that on to me and my brothers. She worked all her life from the time she was twelve. When my parents became owners of Community Disposal Service in Corning, I recall both of them working long, hard hours to make that business the success it eventually became. It was not unusual to see Mom drop off to sleep on the living room couch at 10 or 11 at night with the business books or papers spread on her lap and a pen or pencil in her hand.

Dad drove one of the trucks, the one that picked up the hoppers from businesses. It was called the "load lugger truck." He took care of the employees and set up their routes, and he worked hard, too. But for all my parents' hard work, I'm convinced the business would not have made a dime if Mom hadn't been there to oversee both the business and family finances. When Dad had money, he spent it. Mom was the saver in the family, the investor. Together, they were a terrific team.

Just one thing bothers me now. Since Mom died, I've had this nagging feeling that I never properly mourned her passing. Oh, I did what I could to help at the time, and I mourned for those few days. But I don't think I ever slowed down enough to properly mourn after that initial period from her death to her funeral. I cried for her then, but I haven't cried for her since. I need to do that. I tell myself that one day I will.

Rest in peace, Mom, until we see each other again, as always, when this journey I'm on has ended. I will always love you.

CHAPTER 35:

TO THE BRINK

Maybe because I was the oldest of the three children, I picked up a lot of Mom's strengths and characteristics. For example, she was frugal; I'm frugal (though some just call me cheap). She had business smarts; I think I've shown that I do, too. Whatever the problem, she seemed to have the answer; I've had to find the way out of many a family crisis since her passing.

When Lillian Clark died on November 26, 1997, Dad and us boys dealt with our grief in different ways. Looking back, I feel that we were all in a state of shock. I had lost not only my mother but a best friend. Dad had lost his soul mate, and he could not manage without her. He literally did not know how to write a check, let alone balance a checkbook.

Being the oldest of the boys, I naturally stepped in to handle many of the responsibilities that previously had fallen on Mom. But the job was bigger than any of us could have anticipated. Before we knew it, the events set off by Mom's passing pushed our family to the brink of personal and financial collapse.

Somehow, we made it through that terrible period and emerged safely on the other side. But none of us made it through unscathed.

The trouble started when Dad decided he'd had enough of the garbage business and didn't want to operate Community Disposal

Service without the love of his life, his best friend and his lifelong business partner by his side. He gave the business to Dan and Doug, since they had been working with him and had showed some interest in it.

My brothers operated the business for about another year and a half and then decided to sell it to another local company, Casella Waste Management. They got a good price for it and split the money. Dan used his share to make some smart investments, but Doug made the mistake of buying a burned-out bowling alley in Hornell, a small city located in western Steuben County. Doug and his wife, Irene, put a lot of work into remodeling Hornell Bowl, and when they reopened it, business seemed to be booming.

I don't know what happened next, but there was a sharp reversal and pretty soon the business collapsed. Bowlers stopped coming, but the bills didn't, and before anybody knew it Doug and Irene were deep in debt.

Well, at least one other person knew it, and that was Dad. Unknown to the rest of us, he had co-signed a loan with Doug for the purchase of the bowling alley. And when Doug could no longer meet his financial obligations, Dad began making the monthly loan payments.

The first inkling I had that Dad was in so deep was when Belva Felker, a teller at the bank who had befriended Dad and helped him with his banking, informed me that he owed $11,500 for the previous month's payment. It was already well past due, and the bank's home office was threatening to recall the loan. That would have cost Dad all the collateral he had put up—his entire life's savings.

I had Belva take money to cover the payment from my account. But that was just a quick fix, and a temporary one. This was the beginning of a three-year period that was to be one of the most stressful times of my life.

At the time I made his loan payment, Dad was in the hospital recovering from heart problems. He didn't need the additional stress, so I kept the news from him and didn't discuss the business. But the situation at the bowling alley only worsened, and it was still there, waiting for him, when Dad returned home.

Hornell Bowl eventually closed, and now Dad was making payments on a business that was bringing in no money. I couldn't sit back and watch this happen, so again I jumped in to help. We put the bowling alley up for sale, and while it sat quietly on the market for more than a year, I had what seemed like an endless series of meetings with lawyers, accountants, real estate people, tax consultants and I don't know who all else—all dealing with this business that I should have had nothing to do with.

I didn't need the additional stress any more than Dad did. The realization that I might have to retire from coaching because of the effects of post-polio syndrome was weighing heavily on my mind, and the physical demands of coaching were wearing down my body. The fun seemed to have been drained out of baseball, and it was becoming just a job. The additional worry over Dad's financial dilemma almost seemed too much.

At about that time, Camilla's mom and stepdad started talking seriously about coming to Corning—not to visit but to live. The big question facing them was: What would they do once they got here? Where would they work?

I got the brilliant idea—or so I thought at the time—of starting another garbage collection company. Camilla's stepdad, Per, could work there, receive a small ownership percentage, and eventually take over the business.

I found two partners who wanted to help make this brilliant idea a reality. One was Dad, who would be our main consultant, since he'd been in the business for thirty-five or forty years, whereas I knew nothing about it. (My brothers couldn't help because when they sold Community Disposal Service they signed a five-year non-compete clause.) My other partner was John Princiotti, a friend and my stockbroker.

Being an old baseball guy, I called the new company Diamond Disposal Service. (Probably even non-fans know that a baseball field is called a diamond because of the shape of the infield.) We opened for business in April of 2001, and Per was here to help get Diamond off the ground.

Our first employee was Ray Hanshaw. He was recommended by Dad as somebody who could do it all—drive a truck, service the trucks and generally oversee the operation.

My brilliant idea became just one more burden on my already exhausted body and mind. Now I had the Hornell Bowl situation to deal with, a new business with all the typical start-up problems and growing pains, my coaching work, and the increasing effects of post-polio. Besides, I had now begun working on this book.

Just what was I thinking?

I hadn't been thinking enough of my family, apparently. Without realizing it, I'd begun neglecting Camilla and Elicia. All the demands on me barely left enough hours to sleep, let alone spend some so-called quality time with my wife and daughter.

Camilla confronted me with the facts of the situation one evening. I had just dragged myself into the house, drained of all energy as usual, wanting only to soak in a hot shower for a few minutes and then drop off to sleep. But Camilla made me sit and listen as she spelled out for me what I was too busy to see for myself. She gave it to me straight, and it really opened my eyes. I had no good response, because she was right and I knew it. As I listened to her plea for my attention—to her and to our daughter—I had to agree that I hadn't been a very good husband and father lately. I promised her I'd make it up to them.

From that moment on, I tried to change, I really did.

Despite my best efforts, though, I didn't find more time for my home life. And when I did take a few minutes to sit and talk with Camilla after a long day at work, what I wanted to talk about was getting away from it all—or much of it. What was keeping us in Corning? What was holding us in the Northeast, where the winters were too long? I've always hated the cold, and now, as I was getting older and my body seemed to ache more with the effects of post-polio, I began thinking it was time to pull up stakes and head south.

I'd always liked Florida, with its heat and humidity, and now I began trying to convince Camilla that we should sell our house in Corning and move to Florida. We could find a nice place on the water, I told her. Elicia would love it there. We could enjoy the good life.

She resisted. To her, we *had* the good life. She'd already uprooted her life once, moving from her homeland in Sweden to come live with me in the States. Corning was her home now. She'd made a new life there, made new friends, and she wasn't quite ready to give up all that to move again.

I loved Corning, too, and still do. But I badly wanted to move to Florida, and so we discussed it, sometimes heatedly. Somehow, I convinced Camilla to look at homes in Florida, and eventually we went ahead and bought a house in Cape Coral, on a canal.

It was my dream home. There was just one problem. I wondered, for a time, if I'd be making the move there by myself.

I still had not convinced Camilla that this was best for us. As our moving time approached, the tensions between us neared the breaking point. Camilla actually threatened to leave me. She said she and Elicia would stay behind in Corning and start a life of their own, if necessary. And that hurt me deeply.

I did not want to be without my wife and daughter. That's not what this move was about. I wanted us to move as a family, and I could not imagine doing it alone.

But Camilla and I continued to disagree, and to argue. On top of everything else I was going through at the time, the strain was too much for me. Finally, not long before our scheduled moving day, I decided I had to get away, and so I did. I moved in with Dad and waited out the storm.

The movers showed up as scheduled on December 10, 2003. Here were all these strangers tramping through our house, packing up our belongings and loading them into a large moving van. Camilla and I were going through all the emotions people usually go through on the day they're about to pull up roots, with the additional stress of our now uneasy relationship. And then it only got worse.

Sue, a friend of Camilla's, offered to move our van to give the moving men a clearer path from the house to their truck. But the crash I heard next was her backing the van through our closed garage door. I was ready to leave right then and there.

Somehow, we got through that difficult period.

We moved, all of us, Camilla and Elicia and I. We settled into our new home and found that we loved it, as I hoped we would (and *knew* I would).

"It was tough," Camilla recalls. "I'd already moved a couple of times, and to again move to a city I didn't know, with no people I knew, it's something I really didn't want to do. But it was a dream Dave had, to move to Florida, so I felt I would try it for a couple of years. If it didn't work, we could always move back. We're still here."

Eventually, Dad found a buyer for Hornell Bowl before the business bled him to death financially or stressed him to death physically. For me, it meant a trip back to New York in the summer of 2004 to help close the deal. It made me feel good to see Dad get the opportunity he deserved to finally live the carefree retirement life.

Camilla and I also sold two properties we owned in Corning, in addition to our home there. One was an office building and the other a duplex apartment house.

As for Diamond Disposal, well, that didn't develop quite as expected. After the terrorist attacks of 9/11, when citizenship became tougher to obtain, Camilla's parents decided to continue living in Sweden after all, because Per couldn't get the necessary paperwork done to establish citizenship here.

But just when it looked as if I'd be stuck running the business, my brother Dan bought it from me after his five-year non-compete clause expired. Dan did well with Diamond and even had our brother Doug working for him.

Dan had lived in Tampa for a while after graduating from Corning Community College, where he played baseball for me. He earned a degree in history and geography from the University of South Florida, and met his future wife, Karen, while he was there. She has a daughter, Jerrica, from a previous marriage, and she and Dan have two kids of their own—Brent and Ashley. They eventually moved back to the Corning area and now live in nearby Gang Mills—but separately, since their divorce.

Doug, who never did take to sports, developed talents of his own. He was always mechanically inclined and could do electrical work that just puzzled me. He didn't go to college but instead went to work for Dad at Community Disposal Service, and then for Dan at Diamond. Doug married Irene, from Steuben County, and they have two kids— Kimberly and Kristopher. They live in the Corning area now.

As for Camilla and me, we survived one of the worst summers of hurricanes in Florida's history during our first year in our new home, and more storms the following year. The house sustained severe damage during one of the hurricanes in 2004, and more damage during another in 2005. But fortunately none of us was hurt, and in time the damage was repaired.

I really began to spend more time with my family once we settled into our new home, and life became fun again for all of us. Elicia started kindergarten that first year in Cape Coral, and she joined Girl Scouts and a T-ball league. She's a good baseball player, too. A chip off the old block, if I say so myself. Except she's already a better hitter than her old man ever was.

For three awful years or so, life wasn't much fun for me or for the people closest to me. I feel stronger for having survived that time, but I'm not happy for what it did to my family.

I don't want to ever have to go through anything like that again.

CHAPTER 36:

COACHING COUNTDOWN

The week after Mom died, I signed as a roving coach with Major League Baseball International. I had reached the "show" at last—in some capacity, anyway.

As the name implies, Major League Baseball International is big-league baseball's wide-reaching overseas arm—its eyes and ears wherever baseball is played all over the globe. Not many people know much about it, but they know that lots of foreign players have made their way to the major leagues, and MLBI is where the search for those players begins. Getting a job with that arm of Major League Baseball was a great opportunity, and as a bonus it allowed me to continue as pitching coach for the Swedish Junior National Team, and as a scout for the Atlanta Braves.

The way I got the job with Major League Baseball International just reinforces what I've said about the way things work out for me. A negative turned into a positive, and this cat landed on his feet once again. Here's what happened:

The 1997 European Junior Championships were played in Hull, England, and Sweden won only one game. I was ejected from one of the games for arguing that the other team's batters were diving into pitches to intentionally get hit. Our pitchers had hit four batters, and three of the pitches that hit them appeared to be strikes.

As pitching coach, I went out to make my case. I started yelling at the home plate umpire, but he couldn't speak English and didn't know what I was saying. The ump at first base came running down to get between us.

"Cool it now or you'll get the heave-ho," he said to me.

But I didn't cool it, and before long he gave me the heave-ho.

I must have had a flashback to the days when I went to Dunn Field in Elmira and watched Earl Weaver drive the umpires crazy. Yes, this is the same Earl Weaver who later entertained fans for years as the fiery manager of the Baltimore Orioles. He was managing the Orioles' farm team in Elmira when I saw him in action—and I do mean action. Weaver was famous—or maybe "infamous" is the proper word—for his antics during his many heated arguments with umpires.

In this particular exchange I had with the umpire in the Junior Championships, I didn't cool it even after getting the heave-ho. Instead of just turning and walking away, as I should have, I bent over, scooped up some dirt and tossed it onto home plate. It did no good, of course, but I felt a little better for having done it, and our players and fans loved it.

I went into the clubhouse, changed into street clothes and took a seat in the stands to watch the rest of the game. As it turned out, the man sitting next to me was a major-league scout. We struck up a conversation, and as the game went on he asked if I'd be interested in being a roving coach for Major League Baseball International. I told him I'd think about it and get back to him early in the off-season. When I did so, I told him yes, I'd be interested.

My new job took me back to Sweden and to other countries in Europe as an instructor and scout. I traveled to Finland, the old Czech Republic, Austria, Belgium, Holland and Germany from my base of operations in Falun, Sweden, where Camilla and I had purchased a home during the 1996 season. We also had a home in Corning, which we moved into after the 1997 season. Camilla designed that house and we did a lot of the interior work ourselves, starting the construction in September of 1996. Actually, we were originally scheduled to move into the house the same day Mom died, but we didn't get in until a couple of weeks later, on December 12.

The job with Major League Baseball International was great, and I was honored to be a representative of Major League Baseball. I was assigned to a specific country for a period of time, and to teams in that country, and then I moved on to another country and other teams. I coached the players and offered tips to the managers and coaches, and I put on clinics and gave talks on baseball. And all the while I was scouting for MLBI—looking for talent, for trends in the different countries I visited, for indications of the health of the game of baseball in that part of the world. Daily, I reported on my activities and my findings.

Meanwhile, I was still scouting for the Braves, alerting them to players who showed some promise.

There was a downside to that MLBI job, though: I missed being involved in the games and preparing for the games. I missed watching the standings and the scoreboard. I missed being part of a team. The competitor in me wasn't satisfied.

It helped that I was able to coach with the Swedish Junior National Team again in 1998, when the European tournament was played in Vienna. And it was fun when Sweden pulled a surprise by finishing third that year and taking home the bronze medal. That was the country's best finish in more than twenty years.

The following year, I coached half a season with the Elmira Pioneers, which was now an independent franchise in the Northern League (earlier, and later, they played in the Northeast League, and eventually in the Canadian-American League, before finally ceasing operations). I helped with the pitchers during workouts at Dunn Field and at home games there until I had to leave for Europe again and my second season with Major League Baseball International.

In 2000, I again coached with the Pioneers, this time for the whole season but just at home games and practices in Elmira. We won both halves of the split season in our division and lost to Adirondack, a team from Glens Falls, New York, three games to one, in the second round of the playoffs.

After that season, I decided to take a year off from baseball. I had to see if that would have any effect on my body, if it would do anything to slow the progress of the post-polio syndrome that slowly but surely was weakening me. It was a difficult decision but one that I needed to make and, frankly, one that I probably should have made after the championship season of 1997 with Leksand, if not earlier.

Long before I decided to step away, I knew that the physical demands of coaching were taking their toll on my body. I had stopped throwing batting practice after the 1995 season and stopped hitting fungos (fly balls and grounders during practice) after the 1996 season, except occasionally. And in those past two seasons, coaching with the Elmira Pioneers, I had begun using a scooter to get around the field during the long afternoons of extra instruction and batting practice.

By the time I ended my coaching career, I had cut my workouts from a peak level of about four hours every day to forty-five minutes just three days a week. My routine now consisted of light weights, calisthenics, stretching and a stationary bike ride. Still, I put a lot of stress and strain on my shoulders in the course of a season.

The only reason I didn't get out sooner was that opportunities kept presenting themselves. And I've never been one to pass up an opportunity, or a challenge. Finally, though, as difficult as it was, I had to stop, at least for a while, even though I still had opportunities to continue coaching.

Despite my initial reluctance to get into coaching, I had come to love it. I got a great sense of satisfaction in helping other players develop their skills and broaden their knowledge of the game. Giving that up was almost as difficult as deciding never to play again.

In 2000, the year I stopped coaching (except for the Swedish Junior National Team), I was still scouting, now for the San Diego Padres. And I began doing more motivational speaking, something I'd done on and off for several years. That went well, too: In just three years, I would find myself speaking at the National Post-Polio Convention in Greensboro, North Carolina, and at the Baseball Hall of Fame in Cooperstown.

Denis Sweeney of Corning, who played for me at Corning Community College, joined me as a booking agent for my speaking engagements. He did some research into my career and figured out that I'd been involved in more than six hundred wins in more than thirty years as player, coach and manager. Wow! I really had no idea.

In 2002, Mike Veeck, Bill Veeck's son, dropped me a note asking: "How about Brockton? Would you be interested in it?" He wanted me to coach for the independent team he owned in Brockton, Massachusetts, one of his many baseball projects. Brockton played in the same league as Elmira, so I knew the team and the league and I had a good idea of what I would be getting into if I took the job. Under different circumstances, I think I might have taken it, too, and I told Mike so. I certainly would have enjoyed teaming up with him, and I told him that, too. Reluctantly, though, I had to turn down the offer.

I did return to Sweden that year, though, as a coach for the Junior National Team for one final season. And we won a silver medal that summer at the European Championships, which was played in Sweden for the first time. It was a big thrill for all of us who were involved—especially, of course, those young Swedish players who performed so well on their homeland.

Tony Klarberg was the manager of that club. Other coaches besides me were Jerry Kendall, a former major-leaguer, and Michael Bjorklund. It was my last team as a player, manager or coach.

In that same year, 2002, I saw a specialist, Doctor Richard Bruno, at the Post-Polio Institute in Englewood, New Jersey. I was fifty years old now, and feeling every bit of it and more.

When it came time for Doctor Bruno to tell me what he'd found, he didn't sugar-coat it. He gave it to me straight, and I've always liked that approach, even if what I had to hear wasn't very pleasant. And this wasn't very pleasant.

The doctor said that if I didn't start paying attention to what my body was telling me, then within five years I would experience excruciating pain just getting through my normal daily routine. He told me what I had to do to have any hope of avoiding that: I needed to use a wheelchair or scooter to move around, ride a power chair on stairs, and install ramps at my home.

Well, how could I argue with the man? Everything he said made perfect sense, and I should have done as he suggested—more than suggested: *urged*. In fact, I should have done it years ago.

I should have, but it was a few years yet before I finally did.

CHAPTER 37:

OUR NEW LIFE

I'm pretty set in my ways. As I write this, I still don't use a wheelchair, and only recently have I started riding a scooter regularly to get around. Call me a work in progress.

Stupid pride kept me from using the scooter sooner. Sometimes I feel as if people are looking at me differently when they see me in a wheelchair or scooter. Maybe it's just me, I don't know.

When I started my athletic career I was on crutches and it didn't bother me because the crutches had always been part of me. That's who I was. But a wheelchair or a scooter? That was altogether different.

The adjustment has been made easier by a change of location for the Clarks. In late 2003, Camilla, Elicia and I made the move to Cape Coral, Florida.

I have spent so much time in Florida over the course of my life that it had long ago become something of a second home. Our baseball camp was there, I scouted there, and I went to spring training and played games for many years all over the state. So I felt comfortable from the day we moved into our new home.

And I felt comfortable using my three-wheel electric scooter to get around, too—still do, in fact. And that's a good thing, because I need it now more than ever. What a Godsend it has been. It's allowed me to continue going to a lot of places and doing many things that I wouldn't be able to go to or do without it.

I just don't have the energy I used to have, because of age and, more importantly, post-polio. Now I must prioritize my energy output every day, and using the scooter rather than walking a distance is one way I do that.

When we lived in Corning, I resisted using the scooter because I was too well known around the area as "Dave Clark, the amazing athlete." I couldn't go anywhere in the Corning-Elmira area without someone engaging me in a conversation about baseball. That's nice, and I've always enjoyed those talks. But as I got older and my energy level declined, something as simple as stopping to talk for a while could become taxing—physically, I mean, because of the need to support myself on crutches.

I remember riding in my scooter one day in Corning. A man came up to me and started talking baseball. He obviously knew who I was, but I didn't know him. After a while he looked at me funny, as if he'd just noticed my means of transportation, and he said, "Hey, you getting lazy in your old age?"

Brother, that did it. The scooter went into storage right after that and didn't come out for quite a while. I wasn't going to have people think I'd become lazy, dammit.

Of course, I shouldn't be embarrassed to use my scooter, and now I'm not. In Cape Coral, I don't have any image to live up to. The friends and acquaintances I've made in my new hometown know me as a guy who uses crutches *or* a scooter to get around. And the people who don't know me generally accept my limitations and the fact that I look different doing some things, and that I might do some things in an unconventional way. Maybe they understand that the unconventional way is the only way that works for me.

I'll point out here that because I've often had to find my own way of doing things, I've been very tolerant, as a coach, of other people's varying approaches to certain tasks. Many coaches instruct their players to do things this way or that way—and, in fact, most baseball organizations encourage coaching that turns out an entire system of pitchers, for example, who throw with a nearly identical delivery. I've heard Tom Seaver, the Hall of Fame pitcher who later was a commentator on baseball telecasts, talk about this as the "cookie-cutter" approach to coaching. Tom hates it, and so do I.

When I'm working with a player, there are only two reasons why I'll tinker with the way he does things, whether it's hitting or pitching or fielding or whatever. One is if he asks for help because he's struggling. The other is if I feel he's doing something wrong—not just different, but wrong—and could do it better with a slight change in his mechanics.

If what he's doing works for him, I leave him alone. I don't care if he's standing on his head while doing it. I won't change a thing no matter how unconventional or silly he might look. The thought is always in the back of my mind that when I played I certainly took an unconventional approach to almost everything I did, and to some other people I probably looked silly.

And not only when I played baseball. I've had to approach many everyday tasks in life in my own special way. If people thought I looked silly, I've always felt that was their problem, not mine. I'd faced my problem and overcome it; if they couldn't deal with that, well, tough. Those people have always been there, from the kids who picked on me in school to the fans who heckled me from the stands, to the few teammates who couldn't accept me as an equal.

I'm still confronted with that attitude sometimes. I remember a few months after we arrived in Cape Coral, I encountered a pea-brained redneck who happened to be driving a pickup truck across one of the intracoastal waterway bridges from Cape Coral to Fort Myers the same time I was out for a drive with Dad, who had come down for a visit. As we approached the Fort Myers side of the bridge, I slowed for a red light up ahead and I noticed the pickup speeding up behind me. As I watched, the driver swerved to the right, taking the inside on the six-lane approach. He flew by us and then came to a screeching halt at the light.

When I pulled up next to him, I could see him shaking his head, a scowl on his fat face. Then he turned and gave me a sideways sneer, still shaking his head. I lowered the window on the passenger side, where Dad was sitting, and called out, "Do you have a problem with me?"

He went into a rant, cursing and yelling that I was a terrible driver and if I wanted to go ten miles an hour I should stay to the right lane. Well, people who have ridden with me know that I can get over the highway pretty good. Look, I don't go around bragging about this, but I'm a guy who, as a student at Ithaca College, got two speeding tickets within six days—for speeds of ninety-one and eighty-seven miles an hour. My license was suspended, and I should stop right here, but I'll tell you what I did next just because it's so crazy it makes me shake my head today to think of it. I went across the state line from Corning to Pennsylvania, got a driver's permit, took the driver's test in Wellsboro and received a Pennsylvania license. That was fine until the folks at the national license center in Washington discovered what I'd done. I had to forfeit my Pennsylvania license and a substantial amount of money to make things right.

That was not typical of me, though. And nowadays I don't generally speed at all, but I don't clog up traffic, either. I consider myself a sensible driver, and when I approach a red light I slow down. Obviously, this guy and I had different driving instructors.

We jawed with each other through that red light, and at some point this guy apparently noticed that my van was equipped with a hand brake. All of a sudden he started calling me a "crippled bastard" over and over again. Then, thankfully, the light turned green and he was gone in a screech of rubber.

I felt violated by the verbal attack. Worse, I was sorry that Dad had to be a witness to it. It hurt me, and I know it hurt and embarrassed him. But more than hurt, I was angered.

Who did this guy think he was? What made him so special? And even if he was special—which, trust me, he wasn't—what made him think he could talk that way to someone who did nothing more offensive than slow down for a red light?

If that lughead reads this—and I'm assuming here that he *can* read—I'm sure he'll recognize himself. My message to him, and to others like him, is that it's you who should be pitied, not me. You must have no self-respect if you can take satisfaction from verbally attacking someone with obvious physical limitations simply because he has obvious physical limitations. You probably can't even understand this, but I would not trade places with you for anything in the world.

I only thank God there are not more people like you.

Mostly, I love our new life. I have everything that I've longed for.

We live in my dream home in a community that is everything I want at this stage of my life. Our house is perched on the edge of the water, my boat sits on a lift at our dock just off our back yard, and there's a swimming pool and hot tub in our enclosed lanai. We live about a mile from the shoreline of the Gulf of Mexico, and whenever the mood hits, I can drive our boat out into that wide expanse of beautiful turquoise water and fish or just relax.

Besides, I've been able to continue working in baseball. When we moved to Florida, I was a part-time scout for the Baltimore Orioles, the team that gave me my first taste of life in the major leagues as an associate scout. It felt good to complete that circle.

Camilla and Elicia are with me, and it gives Camilla and me great joy and pride to watch our daughter grow.

My only regret is that Mom didn't live to see her granddaughter, and that Elicia didn't get to know her Grandma Clark. I know they would have thought the world of each other, and I take some satisfaction in the feeling that Mom is up there somewhere keeping watch over Elicia with a big, wide smile on her face.

Yeah, I love our new life. What's not to love?

Well, okay, there are the alligators that swim past the house from time to time. And the Nile monitor lizards, which can grow to seven feet in length and which occasionally climb out of the water and walk right up into our back yard. But those are minor inconveniences, and we quickly learned to accept the 'gators and lizards as just some of our new neighbors.

The really difficult part of the adjustment to Florida hit us several months after we moved into our new home. And I mean *hit*—in the form of four hurricanes that battered the state in rapid succession that summer of 2004. Hurricane Charley, in particular, seemed to target Cape Coral and neighboring communities when it struck on August 13.

Camilla, Elicia and I were forced to evacuate our home, along with many other people in Florida, as Charley approached. We felt like nomads, heading to Orlando, about a three-hour drive northeast of Cape Coral. We spent three weeks in hotels, just before and after Charley, and Elicia started back to school while we were still living out of a hotel in Fort Myers. The new school year had started on August 8, but the kids didn't make it through the first week before Charley forced classes to be suspended.

When we finally returned home, the devastation we found was shocking—not just to our home and boat, but to our neighborhood, the entire city and communities all around us. Our house and property absorbed about forty thousand dollars' worth of damage. Charley ripped off shingles and siding and knocked around our new boat. There was damage inside and outside the house, leaving us with an awful mess to clean up when we finally returned home.

The destruction was everywhere, and we held our breath in anticipation as we began seeing signs of it on our drive back from Orlando. Buildings were heavily damaged, trees were uprooted, and signs were knocked down or blown away. In Cape Coral, we were without electrical power for three weeks.

We had two choices at this point: give up and head back north, or pull up our boot straps and get to work fixing what had to be fixed. We chose the latter, of course, and it was a long and arduous process.

There were mornings when Camilla, Elicia and I would be seated at our dining room table, eating breakfast, while carpenters were already hard at work inside our house, sawing, sanding, hammering and whatnot. But finally all that came to an end. The last of the repairs was completed on January 12, 2005—five months, nearly to the day, after Hurricane Charley blew through.

And Charley was just the first of the hurricanes that summer of 2004. Frances, Jeanne and Ivan followed, slamming into Florida one after the other. We would watch their progress on the Weather Channel with considerable concern—one storm moving on past us while another built up strength and speed out in the Atlantic and took aim at our new home state. While none of the other hurricanes had the same devastating effect as Charley, they all were disruptive. Elicia couldn't get a routine going because schools would frequently close for evacuation or because of damage.

It's hard to put into words how devastated the area was. Just as an example, we couldn't waste gas because it was so scarce. Ships couldn't bring the fuel to port for a time, and even when they could, some of the pipelines had been damaged and couldn't carry the gas. Long lines of vehicles formed at the gas stations that had supplies, and tempers sometimes flared. By the time Ivan skirted us, many people had had enough, and some simply put their homes up for sale and moved back up north.

A little over fourteen months after Charley, we found our home again in the bull's eye of a hurricane. This time, on October 24, 2005, Wilma whipped across Florida, and again we evacuated to Orlando as she drew near.

Wilma was a category-three hurricane with winds of a hundred and twenty-one miles an hour when she crashed into Cape Coral. The impact on our home this time was not as extensive, but it still cost us many thousands of dollars in repairs. The damage was limited to the exterior of the house—part of the roof and a screened enclosure on the pool were ripped up, and there was some damage to our dock—but at least our boat was spared.

It will take years for our area to fully recover from the storms. But I have no doubt that it will get there. Although I wasn't home when the Flood of '72 struck the Corning area, the devastation that I found when I returned was somewhat like what I now saw in Florida. That's why I know we'll be all right. Corning and communities in that area bounced back, and we will too.

Still, each time I hear of a storm taking aim at our part of Florida, I think of a conversation I had with the real estate agent who sold us our house. On the day of the closing, I asked her, "What's the hurricane situation like here?"

"Oh, don't worry about that," she said. "We haven't taken a direct hit here in forty years."

And I thought, *Oh, God, law of averages.*

CHAPTER 38:

WORDS OF WISDOM

Sometimes when I look back on my life, I wonder, *"Was that really me? How did I accomplish that?"*

Most of those things happened in the world of baseball, but not all. I've already written about how I played hockey, how I bowled, how I've fished and gone boating, and how once I had a hole-in-one while golfing. But I've also been parasailing in Mexico, which gave me a breathtaking view, from four hundred feet up, of stingrays swimming in the clear blue Caribbean. I've gone snow skiing up north, using my crutches as ski poles, and snorkeling in the Grand Cayman Islands. And I've gone whitewater rafting with Camilla down a mountain stream in Jamaica, pulling a large banana leaf over our heads for cover when it started raining.

There hasn't been much that I wouldn't at least try, and my life has been so much richer for it.

One thing I've learned is that baseball, and sports in general, mirrors life and is a great training ground for life. Any lesson you learn in sports is something you can apply to any other endeavor in your life.

To succeed in sports you need desire, determination, passion, toughness, perseverance, motivation, teamwork, accountability, responsibility, confidence; intense focus over the long haul, a positive mental attitude and a strong work ethic. The same principles apply to anything you might do in life.

I see baseball, and life, as a pyramid. Many play at the bottom of the pyramid, but fewer and fewer compete at each level as you climb the pyramid. And the higher you climb, the more work is required not only to stay there but to continue climbing.

Life is a series of decisions. So are the games we play. The key is to make more good decisions than bad ones.

I'll offer this advice: Before you make a decision, think the situation through thoroughly, and consider the impact your decision will have on others as well as yourself. This will prepare you to go on to your next decision, your next step in life.

The older we get, it seems, the more cynical and hardened we become about many things in our lives. The same is true of sports. As young athletes, we are bright-eyed and bushy-tailed. We're confident and cocky, and our job is to play children's games and, hey, get paid for it. But too soon we realize that the game stole our heart and, in too many cases, it threw our heart on the ground and stomped on it.

The "chosen few," among which I count myself, go on playing at higher levels, but only for a short while longer. The less fortunate are stopped by lack of skill or lack of mental discipline and/or determination. Injury or Father Time finally catches up with the rest of us. We all lose our innocence over time and become hardened to life's, and sport's, hard lessons.

I just wanted to share that and some other thoughts with you as a way of wrapping up this story of my life. If you find some wisdom here, or some inspiration, then great. If not, then please excuse the amateur philosophy.

Here goes:

Good coaches and good teachers have a lasting effect on your life. You'll remember them as long as you live—their names, their faces and their voices—though it may be years before you begin to realize what an impact they had on your development as a person and as an athlete or whatever you become.

I hope there are people who, when they think of the coaches who have helped them succeed, think of Dave Clark.

Anticipate. In baseball, that means thinking ahead two or three innings. Be ahead of your opponent mentally by anticipating all the possibilities before the next play happens. Then, when it happens, you can react, like leafing through a file folder and pulling out the right response.

The same theory can be applied to so many things in life.

Don't be afraid of making mistakes. We all make them. But when you make a mistake, learn from it and try not to make the same mistake again. Then forget it and move on. If you don't, you'll be playing not to lose rather than playing to win.

I've always tried to take good care of my body. I was and still am a fitness fanatic. I never smoked, did drugs or drank excessively. Yes, I've been drunk on occasion, mostly at celebrations of one kind or another, but not often. Generally, I've lived a very clean lifestyle, and because of that I'm in pretty good health today for guy in his fifties.

The post-polio is doing its thing on me, but I have no control over that. Still, rarely do I go to a doctor, and I'm not on any medication whatsoever.

I'll never understand the athlete who abuses his or her body, especially with the astronomical amounts of money to be made in sports today. Athletics taught me the value of keeping your body in shape for as long as you can.

I'm different. If I didn't already know that, it would be made very clear to me by the stares I get from children when I walk past them on crutches. After I go by, I can feel them watching me. Sometimes I'll turn and smile or wave to them. This brings about one of two reactions. Either they'll smile in return, and visibly relax, or they'll run and cling to their parents. Does this bother me? Not usually, but it can make me very uncomfortable, depending on where I am, who I'm with and how I'm feeling at that particular time.

Most people fear things that are different, aren't comfortable around them and don't like them. Things that are different don't conform to our definition of "normal."

I've spent my whole life trying to fit in, trying not to look different. Sometimes it just doesn't work.

Baseball, and sports in general, was a way for me to feel free from my disability, from my "different" look. When I was on a baseball field, for example, I felt that my movements were like all the athletes' movements I'd ever seen. I was running just like them, throwing just like them, catching just like them—at least in my mind. When I first had a chance to watch myself on film, I was surprised to see that some of my movements did look quite different.

Over the years, I kept noticing that people, including teammates, would kind of look at me out of the corner of their eyes at first. Once they saw that I could get the job done, they didn't seem to notice or care anymore that my movements were at times a bit unorthodox. I was one of them, a member of the human race. I had passed that test.

Eventually, I became not only accepted but respected for what I did and how I did it. How *could* a guy with crutches, a leg brace and those unorthodox movements succeed in professional sports, and against so-called able-bodied competition? Succeeding and earning people's respect made me feel important. I was doing something that inspired and motivated others.

I've always been a loner, even though I've never lacked for company. I'm naturally an introvert, though I've learned how to be an extrovert through all my experiences in life. Still, I'm basically shy and self-conscious about my appearance, and I wonder what people will think of me when we meet for the first time. Often now, if I'm going to get together for the first time with somebody I've never met, I'll explain on the phone that I walk with crutches or that I use a scooter. I figure that way the other person will be able to form some idea of what I might look like, and I find that I'm more relaxed as I prepare for our first encounter.

I don't like being in big crowds or standing in front of them. That might sound strange for someone who was a professional athlete and who now earns a living partly from public speaking, but I never enjoyed the spotlight.

I like my privacy. It helps that I never get bored. I can always find something to do to pass the time. I'm an avid reader, and I love to watch movies and listen to music. That's how I relax when I'm away from the ballpark.

Nothing relaxes me like being *at* the ballpark, though. For as long as I can remember, I always wanted to be at the park as soon as the gates opened—much sooner, of course, if I was playing, coaching or managing. As a spectator, I find the ballpark is exciting, and yet relaxing, from the minute batting practice starts until the last pitch is thrown.

A ballpark has its own flavors, its own smells: freshly mowed grass, hot dogs with mustard, popcorn, peanuts and spilled beer.

Take me out to the ballgame. And I mean any ballgame. I can have as much fun at a Little League field as at a major-league stadium. It's all about the game.

The brain is the most important muscle in the body. If you think you can, and you prepare yourself, then you have a chance to accomplish anything you set out to do. You'll have confidence, and confidence can help you achieve the impossible, or what you thought was impossible. Confidence allows your body to relax, and your talents shine more naturally when you're relaxed.

It's okay to be scared, nervous and uptight before a game or competition of any kind. But don't ever let fear hold you back. Let it motivate you. Let it spur you on. Let it drive you to perform at your highest level.

Every time I stepped onto a playing field I was scared. More than anything, I feared losing. If you don't fear losing, then the losing means nothing. The fear of losing, of failure, has driven me my entire life, and not just in my career. When I lose, I take it personally, and I feel less important, less of a man.

I've had three major "down" periods in my life—the arm injury and the end of my pitching career, the onset of post-polio syndrome and the end of my playing career, and my mom's death. If those periods taught me anything, it's that the human spirit is resilient. With some effort and the passage of time, we can bounce back from the down times that are certain to hit all of us.

It's not easy to work through those downers. Sometimes we don't even want to; we're ready to give up. But remember: You're not the only one to ever go through what you're experiencing at the moment. And remember this, too: When you work through that depression, you will be stronger for it, and wiser.

Never, ever give up. Believe that you can accomplish any goal you set your mind to, as long as you're willing to put in the hard work that's required and you have a passion for what you're trying to accomplish. But don't expect instant gratification. Be willing to take small steps toward your goal, one after the other.

Keep this in mind: No dream is impossible. And live your life as if you truly believe it. That's the way I approached life, and chances are you have more physical tools to work with than I ever had.

Chapter 39:

Final Thoughts

I know my life is headed for a not-so-glorious end. I know I will be in trouble in my final years. I'm just not sure what that means, exactly.

I have heard others with post-polio talk about being so worn out that they couldn't take another step. They refer to it as "hitting the wall." When I heard that, I couldn't relate, because I hadn't experienced any of what they had. I still haven't hit the wall, but I've experienced enough of post-polio's symptoms that now I can relate. I can see myself getting there.

I'm probably one of the youngest polio survivors. Once my generation is gone, there will be no need for any further research into post-polio, because there will be no more polio survivors. Because of that, I hold out little hope that a cure for post-polio will ever be found.

In a way, the Salk vaccine doomed the people like me who already had polio. No doubt it saved many people who otherwise might have gotten polio, but by wiping out the disease, the vaccine diverted the attention of science and medicine to other diseases and other causes.

If someone were to find a cure for post-polio, I'd be the first in line to sign up for it. I've never taken drugs or other medications, but if a wonder drug came along I'd take it every day if I thought it would help me. Surgery? I've done it before; I certainly would do it in this case.

247

Look, I don't expect to live forever. Nobody is that foolish. I would just like to be around long enough to watch my daughter grow up to become a woman. What parent wouldn't wish for that?

No matter what happens, though, I've been blessed in my life. I've been able to accomplish so much, see so much, meet so many people, be a member of championship teams and even last-place teams. I've talked with presidents, been honored nationally, and traveled across more of the world than I ever dreamed I'd see.

It's been tough at times, sure. But all in all, it's been a great ride.

Dave's Statistics

Pitching

Year	Team	Wins	Losses	Saves	ERA
1971	Hunnewell, Mo.	3	1	0	3.01
1972	Hunnewell, Mo.	4	3	1	4.94
1973	Ft. Lauderdale, Fla.	1	0	2	1.73
1975	Indianapolis Clowns	4	0	20	3.57
1976	Indianapolis Clowns	0	1	1	9.74
1977	Beeville, Tex.	0	0	0	3.00
1977	Pennington, N.J.	9	4	3	2.69
1979	Chesire, Conn.	1	1	0	5.73
1980	Clayton, N.J.	5	4	3	4.03
1980	Delaware Valley	1	0	0	0.00
1981	Rattvik, Sweden	2	1	1	2.56
Career		30	15	31	3.31

Hitting

Year	Team	AB	Hits	RBI	Avg
1971	Hunnewell, Mo.	15	4	1	.267
1972	Hunnewell, Mo.	28	7	0	.250
1975	Indianapolis Clowns	22	3	4	.136
1984*	Indianapolis Clowns	82	13	5	.159
1985*	Indianapolis Clowns	109	28	6	.257
1986*	Indianapolis Clowns	94	25	4	.266
1987*	Indianapolis Clowns	123	37	12	.301
1988*	Indianapolis Clowns	121	34	6	.281
Career		594	151	38	.254

With courtesy (designated) runner

Awards and Honors

1975—Received the Fireman of the Year award as the top relief pitcher for the Indianapolis Clowns.

1977—Inducted into the Corning-Painted Post Sports Hall of Fame; selected a ?rst-string goaltender on the Southern Tier Hockey Association All-Star Team; selected ?rst-team goaltender on the Crystal City Classic Cup All-Tournament Team.

1981—Selected to the Swedish Elite Baseball League All-Star Team as a pitcher.

1996—Received a national Giant Steps Award for coaching, sponsored by Northeastern University's Center for the Study of Sport in Society. It was presented at a dinner in Boston. A few months later, President Bill Clinton welcomed the award winners to the White House.

1997—Named manager of the Northern Division in the Swedish Elite League All-Star Game. Later, was voted runner-up for the Manager of the Year award after leading the Leksand Lumberjacks to the regular-season and playoff championships.

1999—Received the Sporting Goods Manufacturers Association's National Heroes of Sport Award, which was presented at a breakfast in Atlanta, Georgia. Most of the ?nancial award was donated to the Corning YMCA to continue operating the Southern Tier Baseball Camp for the Physically and Mentally Challenged, which Sal Tombasco and I started in 1991.

2001—Received the Corning Community College Distinguished Alumni Award.

2002—Inducted into the Ithaca College Athletic Hall of Fame.

2011—Bo Jackson Courage Award winner.

2011—Paul Harris Fellow - Rotary International award recipient.

Acknowledgments

I want to acknowledge everyone who has helped me along the way, and specifically those who have had a role in bringing my life story to the printed page.

That includes the people I've dedicated this book to, especially my parents, Bernard and Lillian Clark, who were behind me every step of the way, and my wife, Camilla, and our daughter, Elicia, for being such good sports when baseball or the writing of this book took me away from them. And also Roger Neumann, who helped me find the words to tell this story, and to his wife, Nancy, for her understanding of the time it took him to do that.

I want to thank Linda Campbell, the secretary at Diamond Disposal in Corning, New York, for the time she spent typing and copying for me, and for her support of this project. Also Doug Cornfield for his support, and Denis Sweeney, who was there at the beginning and who helped me develop a new career as a motivational speaker.

And I wish to acknowledge my second-grade gym teacher, William Schnetzler; my first Little League coach, Phil Ritz; and my high school gym teacher, Joseph Corcoran. Also Lou Haneles, my coach and mentor; George Long, former owner of the Indianapolis Clowns, a mentor and friend; and Art Gaines, the Pittsburgh Pirates scout who gave me a chance to play professional baseball and helped me develop the confidence that I could succeed.

The authors also wish to thank Ron Lindensmith, our cover designer and photo editor, for the many hours he spent preparing the photo pages; Doug Cornfield, for his advice and assistance throughout the preparation of this book; Denis Sweeney and Sweeney Enterprises; Dan Clark, Dave's brother and the owner of Diamond Disposal Services; and Rocco Shiraldi for their valuable contributions to the project.

Dave Clark